Newfoundland Tr

CW01647469

Vol 3

Taking care of your Newfoundland

Nutrition, common diseases and general care of your Newfoundland

Expertengruppe Verlag

Newfoundland Training

Vol 3

Taking care of your Newfoundland

Nutrition, common diseases and general care of your Newfoundland

EXPERTEN
GRUPPE
VERLAG

TABLE OF CONTENTS

ABOUT THE AUTHOR

Claudia Kaiser lives with her husband and dogs Danny (2 years old) and Daika (8 years old), in an old farmhouse in beautiful Rhineland, Germany.

At first only as a dog owner, but later and after 20 years actively training dogs, she has gained a lot of experience, helping other people to train their Newfoundlands. She formed the idea of writing this book in order to reach more people, than she could have in the local dog training schools and the small circle of dog owners to whom she gave personal coaching.

The publishing of this guide book is the fruit of considerable research, writing and editing. It is designed to be a guide for all budding Newfoundland owners, to help them get the difficult task of training right the first time, and to avoid those mistakes, which Claudia herself made at the beginning. She worked through her own bad experiences over the years, so that the reader does not have to.

Those who follow the tips and tricks covered in this guidebook are sure to have many years of pleasure from these unusual and wonderful companions.

PREFACE

Congratulations! You are lucky enough to share your life with a Newfoundland dog, or you are close to making that choice. This beautiful and memorable breed will fulfil your days and soon you will not be able to imagine life without your four-legged friend.

It has been scientifically proven that taking care of dogs has a positive effect on humans. You will notice it yourself when you automatically begin to light up and be happy when your Newfoundland dog greets you, tail wagging, after a long day at work. Does it not help you to relax when your dog lies snoring in front of the couch while you watch a film?

Dogs are real stress killers for us people. Their honest love for us makes us feel better and happier, besides the incentive that every dog owner has to go out into the fresh air and ideally move around much more than those who do not own dogs. Even those who are chronically ill have confirmed that they feel better having a dog. Your four-legged friend is therefore a real bonus for your health.

It is exactly for that reason it is important you take care of the health of your Newfoundland. Hence the German saying “If the dog is healthy, the human is happy”. It is particularly important for you to take care of him because your dog is often unable to do it for himself.

Unfortunately, these days many dogs are overbred, which itself is the cause of many diseases and other problems which can overwhelm an unexpecting owner. I recommend strongly that you take care when choosing your dog.

Look at his parents and ask the breeder about diseases which have occurred in the litters up to then. If a puppy is already in poor health when you buy it, you will probably have a lot of problems with him later on. In order to avoid this, you should take care before making your choice and, if necessary, speak to a veterinary surgeon for his advice.

Apart from breeding-related problems, there are also a number of challenges which present themselves due to modern processes and developments which did not exist at the time of their ancestor, the wolf. Therefore, it is often necessary to take certain precautions which may cause those who are not familiar with dogs to shake their heads, using the argument: "A wolf would not need that".

If someone says that to you, I would suggest you ignore him. After all, it is about the well-being of your dog.

With this guide I want to give you the necessary knowledge and self-assurance to keep a watchful eye on your Newfoundland so that you know how to react if something is wrong. If this would happen to you, you would probably react as I did and try everything within my power to take the pain away, but I did not know what to do.

It is not possible to prevent your dog from getting sick, even with this guide. However, what you can do is to ensure that these problems are either noticed early enough or you are able to use your knowledge to prevent them in the first place.

In conclusion, it is important for me to emphasise that this book contains tips and recommendations which I have collected through my own experiences and during general dog training sessions. This guide cannot replace a visit to the veterinary surgeon. It is purely intended to give you some knowledge and recommendations along the way. If your Newfoundland is suffering from acute or long-term problems, you should take him to the vet without delay.

I wish you and your Newfoundland all the best for the future and, above all, good health!

- Chapter 1 -

WHAT YOU NEED TO KNOW ABOUT YOUR NEWFOUNDLAND

Did you know that, according to the World Canine Association (FCI), there are officially more than 350 canine breeds recognised today?

Your Newfoundland dog is only one of many different breeds. Naturally, many have things in common. After all, every dog is a descendent, one way or another, from his remote ancestor, the wolf. You can see it more in some breeds than in others.

In this chapter I would like to give you a brief summary about this fascinating breed, so that you know what you are letting yourself in for when you choose a Newfoundland.

At an average height to the withers of 71 cm and a weight of 68 kg, the Newfoundland definitely belongs to the group of large dogs. It is not surprising to know that his fluffy fur gives him the nickname "bear dog". He gets his enormous power and stamina from his ancestors. As the name suggests, this breed originated on the Canadian Atlantic Island, Newfoundland. Although it is not exactly known how he evolved, it is believed that he comes from a mixture of those dogs which were brought to the island by European sailors and fishermen, and those dogs which were native of Newfoundland. In view of his thick undercoat, it is also assumed that some arctic Husky is part of the mixture. There was a theory that the Newfoundland was crossed with the big, black bear dogs of the Vikings, but this is not really considered plausible.

Irrespective of how he came to exist, his imposing stature, his weather resistance and his extreme love of water make him a favourite with fishermen and sailors alike. This dog was capable of pulling fishing nets or boats out of the water with unerring commitment. His tirelessness, despite appalling conditions, made him a popular working dog well outside the confines of Newfoundland. He is often used as a lifeguard, due to his great love of water.

His character makes him less of a bear and more like a sheep. He is always relaxed, peaceful and very lovable. His loyal and good-natured eyes say all you need to know about his character, and despite his size, he is perfectly suited to family life. He loves children and develops strong relationships with them over the years. Due to his size, it is advisable not to leave him on his own with small children. He is not only playful with children, but also shows a great deal of consideration and patience with them. He hardly ever shows any aggressive behaviour and you rarely hear him barking. Perhaps it is his imposing appearance which prevents adversaries from daring to approach, making any barking superfluous. However, if anyone in his pack is in danger, even this peace-loving Newfoundland dog would not hesitate to protect his loved ones.

He loves close contact to his humans and wants to be part of family life. Regular strokes and attention are just as important for him as regular exercise. This big dog does not really feel comfortable with apartment life, he really needs lots of space and is particularly happy near the sea or other waters. You would not be able to pass any stretch of water without allowing him to have a short bath. This intelligent working dog needs fresh air and a lot of exercise every day and that means that his owners must be very active too. He should also be intellectually challenged every day as he is used to solving everyday problems independently.

The Newfoundland is suitable for beginners, due to his quiet and relaxed character. It is important that his training is carried out with loving consistency, a lot of patience and sensitivity. Due to his size, it is important that you set great value in his training. You need to be clear from the start that you will never be able to take a Newfoundland anywhere on the lead if he does not want to go. Therefore, it is imperative that you practice walking him on the lead and calling him back with a great deal of consistency. If he does not obey your commands, you will not be able to control him later.

Now you can see what a wonderful breed you have chosen! On the following pages you can find a short portrait of the breed, according to the FCI standard.

These pages are not enough to give you a full picture of this magnificent animal. However, I hope I have been able to draw you a picture of what it is like to own a Newfoundland. Of course, there are always dogs which do not conform to this description and some have much stronger or weaker characteristics, but I hope that you are able to recognise your Newfoundland in this description.[1]

---

[1] If you would like to find out more about the upbringing and training of your Newfoundland, I recommend that you read the first two books in this series. You can find more information about those books at the end of this one.

Short breed portrait according to the FCI:

Picture	
Country of Origin	Canada (Newfoundland)
Character	Happy, adventurous, lovable, easy-going, majestic, sympathetic and gentle.
Height at withers	Males: approx. 71 cm Females: approx. 66 cm
Weight	Males: approx. 68 kg Females: approx. 54 kg
General Appearance	Solid dog with strong, muscular body.
Eyes	Relatively small, deeply set, wide apart
Ears	Relatively small, triangular with rounded edges, lying flat on the face.Colour: Black, white-black, brown
Fur and Fur Colour	Hair: Water-resistant stock hair. Medium length

	top coat, straight, not curly, soft with dense undercoat. Colour: Black, white-black, brown
FCI-Classification	Group 2: Pinscher und Schnauzer, Molossoid, Swiss Mountain Dog Section 2.2: Molossoid, Mountain Dog
Utilization	Sledge dog for heavy loads, watchdog.

- Chapter 2 -

FUNDAMENTALS OF NUTRITION

In this chapter you will discover what you need to know about feeding your dog. Firstly, I will explain some recommendations for healthy eating and then go on to explore the various types of food available today, such as commercially processed food, raw feeding, home-cooked food, vegetarianism and veganism. After that we will look into what you need to know regarding the feeding of your Newfoundland.

In conclusion, we will touch on a subject which is underrated by many: The water consumption of your Newfoundland. Only too often, owners fail to provide enough fluids for their dogs. I will give you some tips on how you can encourage your dog to drink more.

BASIC RULES FOR FEEDING

It may sound a bit surprising at first, but it is not so important what you feed your dog, but how. For this reason, you will discover in this chapter how you should be feeding him. There are many details which dog owners do not know about and because of that they often harm their dog's health or make their training much more difficult.

It is important to emphasise at this point that these tips are the result of my own training and experience, extensive research and many conversations with other dog trainers. If you have concerns about the methods, I recommend that you speak about them with your vet.

One of the most common questions which I am asked, and which is generally discussed intensively, is how often to feed your Newfoundland. My initial answer is always: It depends!

Depends on what?

It depends on the age of your dog, as an example. A puppy would need to be fed about six times a day, slowly reducing the frequency as he gets older.

I recommend that a fully-grown Newfoundland should be fed twice a day. That of course depends on your daily routine and the health of your dog. Feeding healthy dogs once a day should not cause any problems.

You do not need to worry that your dog will get too hungry. It is a mistake to think they are like us humans. A dog does not need to eat several times a day. Once a day is enough. Of course, that does not mean that you cannot give him some treats in-between. On the contrary, you should continue to give him treats during his daily training sessions, but remember to count the amount that you use as part of his daily food intake. On days where you feed a lot of treats you should reduce the amount he gets in his main meals and vice versa. Failure to do so will result in him putting on more pounds than are good for him.

If you do not feel comfortable with feeding one to two times a day, you can feed your dog more often than he needs if you like, as long as you do not change the amount of food you give him.

It is not unusual, particularly with working dogs, for them to have regular fasting days. This is in compliance with the feeding habits of your dog's ancestors and at the same time ensures that he uses up surplus reserves. I do this with my dogs. Think about it!

A further tip that I have for you is that feeding can be an indirect way of pulling rank. What do I mean by that? Not only with wolves, but also in every pack of dogs, there are specific rules and processes which show, to those who understand them, which dog has which rank among them. Understanding these subtleties will make the training of your dog much easier.

Always give your dog his food last. All the other "pack members" should be finished before he gets his food.

It is important that your Newfoundland does not tuck straight into his food but waits for the command to do so. The best way to do that is for him to take up a sitting position while you calmly put his bowl on the ground, wait a few seconds (or later a little longer) until you give him the command "eat".[2]

It may seem strange to many people, but using this indirect rank pulling, you will rise in rank in the mind

---

[2] You will discover how to give these commands and many more in my guide "Newfoundland Dog Training – Dog Training for your Newfoundland puppy". You will find more information on this subject at the end of the book.

of your dog. In addition, you will avoid your Newfoundland trying to defend his food from you. Often, owners find themselves being growled at if they come close to the dog's full bowl. You can avoid this by practising this exercise every day and showing that you are the boss over his food.

A further and underrated aspect of feeding is the place. Unfortunately, some owners believe that their dogs should be fed in a quiet and secluded spot where it will not be disturbed. Of course, it is important that your Newfoundland is left in peace to eat his food. During this time, children should not be allowed to pester him or urge him to play. However, wolves also never eat completely alone. They are always in sight and calling distance of their pack. Choose a place where he can eat undisturbed but where he is in contact with the rest of the family. In this way, he is involved in family life but learns that it is not a problem when people are close him or walk past him while he is eating. As surprisingly as it may seem, dogs who are used to eating alone can become aggressive if someone suddenly gets close to them. Follow my tip from the very start and you will avoid that.

Once your dog has finished eating, I recommend taking away his bowl immediately, no matter whether there is something in it or not. Why is this tip so helpful? On the one hand, you get your dog used to eating all his food. This is useful if you are in a hurry. On the other hand, this is also an indirect form of pulling rank. This way, you teach him that he can only eat when you (the pack leader) allow it. If you allow your dog to finish his food in his own time, you undermine your own position.

I suggest giving him a quiet time after feeding. Your Newfoundland should not be running around or jumping for at least an hour after he has eaten. A quiet walk, to allow him to relieve himself is quite safe but jumping and running should be avoided at all costs. Why? Your dog's stomach is obviously full after feeding and when he moves around quickly, this can cause a gastric torsion (also known as a twisted stomach), which in 15 to 45 percent of cases can be deadly. You can read about how to recognise a twisted stomach and what to do about it in Chapter 4 – Common Diseases.

In conclusion, I would also advise you not to change the food your dog is eating. Every change can lead to gastrointestinal disorders. This not only applies to changing from dry to wet food but also to the brand or type of food you give your dog. A change of flavour in your dog's feed, however, is not considered to be problematic. Do not worry that you dog may become bored with eating the same food every day. He will not! It is much more challenging for him to get used to new foods on a regular basis. You should carry out any changes on an incremental basis. This means you should start very slowly and change only a small amount of the new food in place of the old. You can increase the amount slowly until, after about 3 to 4 weeks, you have completely replaced the feed.

If your Newfoundland is a poor eater, I recommend checking the temperature of the feed. If the wet food is too cold, for example, because you have just taken it out of the fridge or the dry food is soaked in cold water, it could be unpleasant to eat. Take care to ensure that the food you give him is always at room temperature. I suggest soaking dry food for at least 10 minutes beforehand to enable it to develop its flavour and is not so difficult to eat.

On the following page, I have summarised the points which are most important to consider when feeding your Newfoundland.

Checklist of Feeding Rules:

- ☐ Feeding your dog 1 or 2 times a day is quite sufficient.
- ☐ Your Newfoundland should receive his food last of the family.
- ☐ Before you feed your Newfoundland, you should make him sit and only start eating when you allow it.
- ☐ During feeding, your dog should not be disturbed but should not be too far away from the family.
- ☐ Put the bowl away after feeding is finished, whether or not there is still food in it.
- ☐ Adhere to the quiet time after feeding (at least 1 hour).
- ☐ Do not change the brand or type of food unnecessarily. If it becomes unavoidable, you should introduce him to the new food slowly.
- ☐ Pay attention to the temperature of the food – if it is too cold, it becomes unpleasant for many dogs.

WHEN TO LET YOUR NEWFOUNDLAND MAKE DECISIONS

As mentioned previously on several occasions, your Newfoundland is descended from the wolf. It is important that you understand his descent so that you know what the important things are to consider and how to feed your dog in a consistent manner. As a direct descendent of the wolf, he only differs from his ancestor by 0.1 to 0.3 percent! Did you know that?

What does that mean for you?

The wolf normally only eats unprocessed meat (including offal, bones, fur etc.) and only seldom, when forced to through circumstances, plant-based foods. His teeth are designed for tearing meat and coarsely separating it into pieces. His teeth are not designed to eat ground food (for example grain-based) and the same applies to a typical pet dog of today.

Look carefully into the mouth of your Newfoundland! It differs considerably from your own, which is less designed for tearing and more for grinding and chewing. Your dog seldom chews or grinds his food.

More often he devours smaller pieces without thinking of chewing them.

If you were to ask your Newfoundland, he would instinctively (and genetically triggered) choose unprocessed meat which he could tear apart – quite happily with bone, fur and offal. This is also the case with a typical working dog, such as your Newfoundland.

Newfoundlands enjoy working at their food. The tearing off of pieces of meat or chewing the bone is a real joy and not annoying for your dog, as we humans would perhaps imagine it to be.

However, not everything has remained unchanged with today's pets. As wolves do not know when they will get their next meal, their stomachs can stretch to become extremely big. A fully-grown wolf can eat up to 3 kg of food at once. In comparison, this would be almost 16 kg for an average-sized man of 80 kg! Modern dogs have largely lost this ability, although many dogs tend to eat as much as they possibly can. If you give your Newfoundland as much to eat as he would like, he would become overweight. It is your job to give him just the amount of food that he really needs.

The classical pet dog has become omnivorous (eating all kinds of foods) due to its century-long cohabitation with humans, although he should be given mostly meaty food. Many studies suggest that the nutrition which a modern pet needs differs considerably from that of the wolf. Through centuries of cohabitation with humans, a certain amount of plant-based nutrition has been added to their diet as well as the feeding of dry food or cooked food, which is not thought to be harmful for your pet dog (in contrast to the wolf). It can be seen that not only his behaviour but also his feeding habits have evolved through living with humans, so it is not quite correct to believe that a dog can eat the same as his wolf ancestor. In the next chapter you can read about what could go into his food bowl.

WHAT GOES INTO THE FOOD BOWL?

There are many varying opinions regarding the correct feeding of the modern pet often leading to heated discussions. There are forceful voices supporting every possible method of feeding, which do not allow for contradictions or other opinions.

There are very vocal advocates for all types of nutrition, who are not interested in listening to other opinions.

Jürgen Zentek - Director of the Institute for Animal Nutrition, in Berlin – has a definite opinion on this question:

> "It is basically of no consequence whether the dog is fed cooked food, raw food (including meat and vegetables) or dry food."

This is a statement which may surprise many animal owners. According to Zentek, it does not matter what you feed your dog. More importantly, it should cover his nutritional and energy needs, and ensure that he gets enough minerals, trace elements and vitamins. How he gets them is not important.

On the following pages, I will introduce you to the most common methods of feeding. These will include commercially processed foods, raw foods and home-cooked food. We will also talk about vegetarianism and veganism.

You will discover the pros and cons of feeding processed foods and what you need to be careful of.

In the last sub-section, we will look into what you need to consider when feeding your Newfoundland, compared to other breeds.

COMMERCIALLY PROCESSED FOOD

Although processed foods are often demonised, I think I am not sticking my neck out too far to suggest that it is one of the most common types of pet food used today. In Germany alone, 435 million Euros was spent on dry food, only surpassed by the 473 million Euros spent on wet food during 2018. A further 538 million Euros were also spent on snacks. All of the above belong in the category of commercially processed foods. In total, the sum of 1.4 billion Euros passed over the cashiers' counters.

There are a number of reasons for the enormous popularity of processed foods. These include:

- Its general availability.
- Its simplicity in storage and speed in preparation.
- Its simplicity for working out how much to feed.
- Preparation is carefully state controlled and conforms to the highest standards.

- Experts in the field have calculated the correct amount of vitamins, minerals and trace elements that your dog needs so there is no danger of under or over feeding those.

In short: Commercially processed food is practical! The owner does not need to worry much about anything. However, few people know that we separate processed foods into three separate categories:

- Straight feed material: This is food which consists of a single component and is not meant for feeding on its own. An example of this is the non-mineralised meat tin.

- Supplementary feed material: This is food which consists of at least two components, neither of which are designed to provide all the nutrition a dog needs. Dog biscuits are an example of this, or non-mineralised meat tins with vegetables. With a little experience, the dog owner can make a balanced diet from a mixture of straight and supplementary feed.

- Complete feed material: As the name suggests, this food supplies enough nutrition on its own to cover the needs of your dog.

Unfortunately, there are some processed feed manufacturers who use the latitude of the existing laws to their own advantage and who put their own profits before the well-being of the dog.

If you decide on feeding processed food, it is advisable to check carefully if you are buying a "good" product. I will explain here how you can do that. Take a packet of your dog's food so that you can see what is in it.

Check which type of food you are using. See if it is straight, supplementary or complete. If it is designed as straight or supplementary food, it is possible that your Newfoundland is not receiving all the nutrition he needs.

Next, you should look at the list of ingredients. Interestingly, the law does not require all ingredients to be laid down in writing. If you cannot clearly see the ingredients it is a possible (although not definite) sign that they are not using the best ingredients. Perhaps you need to reconsider your choice of food. Do you not want to know exactly what your dog is eating? And why do the manufacturers not want to tell you what it contains?

Often, manufacturers use descriptions like "chicken flavoured" on their packaging. Have you ever asked yourself how much chicken needs to be present in the food? Here is a short summary:

- "With chicken flavour": In this case, the food must contain more than 0% but less than 4% chicken.
- "Rich in chicken", "extra chicken" or "with extra chicken": These descriptions mean that they must contain at least 14% chicken.
- "Chicken dinner": This means that at least 26% chicken should be present in the food.

The other analytical data mentioned on the packaging is less important in my opinion. The crude protein includes both animal and plant proteins, which differ considerably in both quality and digestibility. In reality, your Newfoundland needs more animal protein, but it is not possible to see how much of it he is getting in this example.

The amount of crude fibre in the package, on the other hand, is important information and something which is underestimated by many. Crude fibre (plant fibre which is difficult to digest or completely indigestible) influences your Newfoundland's stool consistency. It stimulates the digestive system and assists it in its work. I have had very good personal experience with a fibre value of between 1.5 and 2 percent. This value should not be too high as that could be harmful.

The crude fat values on the packaging seem to be as meaningless as the crude protein value as you cannot see which types of fats it includes.

If the crude ash value lies above 5 percent, this could be a sign that it is produced using a lot of feathers and bones. Of course, a wolf eats that and it can provide useful minerals and trace elements. However, I find it hard to believe that these would be present in significant amounts, but they serve as a cheap alternative to valuable lean meat. I would treat feed made from offal, which is advertised as premium quality with caution as it should also contain a sufficient amount of lean meat.

The above was a rough summary of what you should look out for when browsing over the contents of the processed food packaging. It is important that you keep exactly to the recommendations on the packaging. If you only use dry complete feed, you should never add tinned dog food to that. This would cause a surplus to his needs. Keep exactly to the amounts which the manufacturer recommends.

If you are feeding a mixture of straight and supplementary food, I recommend using exactly the amount recommended by animal nutrition experts which can be calculated specifically for your Newfoundland.

RAW FEEDING

The trend towards feeding healthy and natural food does not stop at us humans. More and more owners are trying to feed their dogs as naturally as they can – meaning as closely to the way of the wolf as possible.

The raw feeding method was introduced by the Australian vet, Ian Billinghurst, who has been promoting the use of raw feeding for dogs since 1993. The raw feeding method is known by some as BARF which is short for “bone and raw food”.

Specifically, this means that feeding your Newfoundland would consist exclusively of raw meat, offal, bones and fish. Added to this are fresh fruit, vegetables and nuts which are meant to imitate the stomach contents of the dog’s prey.

The biggest advantage of raw feeding from my point of view is that you know exactly what your Newfoundland is getting to eat and you can ensure yourself of its quality. With normal commercially processed foods, you only see compressed pellets which do not give you any insight as to what they contain, meaning that you have to take the word of the manufacturer.

A further, often overlooked, advantage is that dogs are occupied much longer with their feeding. In most cases it is not possible to devour their food at speed, as with processed foods, because the meat is given in large pieces or whole bones. The dog needs to work to get his food, which may take him some time and this leads to some very active dogs being calmer and more balanced. At this point I would like to discourage you from taking commercial BARF mixtures as they are often already cut into small pieces, which partly diminishes the benefits of the method.

In most cases, BARF food is easier for dogs to digest, particularly those with sensitive digestion or some food sensitivities.

It is not scientifically proven, but many owners believe that the following side effects could be considered positive:

- Better immune system
- Less parasites
- Stronger bones
- Shinier fur

However, despite the advantages of BARF feeding, there are also disadvantages, which can be serious for your Newfoundland. Naturally, the idea of feeding your dog naturally is great, but there could also be dangerous bacteria in the food, parasites in raw meat or it could lead to an under or over supply of nutrients.

Salmonella has often been found in commercial BARF packets. Although dogs with healthy immune systems do not get sick with them, they can pass an infection on through their excrement to their owners or other animals.

To ensure that no parasites are present in raw feed, I recommend buying your meat fresh from the butcher or alternatively freezing it by -20°C so that most parasites are killed off.

Preparing a healthy and balanced diet for your Newfoundland is not easy and probably would not be carried out correctly by the layman. Often there would be insufficient calcium and too much phosphorus, as an example. Also, often the feed does not contain enough vitamin D and iodine. In addition, the ingestion of too much lean meat can be harmful to dogs, causing damage to the kidneys.

If someone were to ask me if I would recommend BARF food, my answer would always be: It depends!

You, as a Newfoundland owner, need to be clear that this method of nutrition takes up a lot more time than feeding processed foods and the costs are usually much higher.

I believe it is absolutely necessary not to feed BARF until you have consulted a vet who is specialised in animal nutrition. You will find a large number of recipes on the internet but few would receive the OK from an expert. No one who has not seen or examined your dog could give you a recipe which contained all the nutrients, minerals and vitamins that he needs at his particular stage of life. Do not allow yourself to be convinced by any online guru.

BARF food yes, but only fed correctly and after consultation with an expert who will examine your dog regularly. I could not, in all honesty, recommend a half-baked solution with pre-prepared BARF feed from a commercial supplier.

To give you an idea of what BARF food looks like, I give below an example for feeding a 65kg dog. Please do not use this on your dog for any length of time if you have not previously consulted an expert.

- 1,040g beef head meat
- 520g boiled potatoes
- 130g shredded carrots
- 13g finely crushed eggshells
- 3,25g Ascophyllum seaweed powder

This recipe needs to be swapped with a different recipe during the week because there is not enough Vitamin D, E and B1 in it to balance your dog's needs.

HOME-COOKED FOOD

The same principle applies to home-cooked food as previously mentioned with BARF food. You, as the owner, have full control over what the dog is given to eat and for that reason, it is important that you speak about the composition of the feed with an expert in dog nutrition.

In contrast to BARF food, however, you would feed your dog little or no raw meat, but would prepare his feed much as you would with a human. An important difference is that your Newfoundland should not be given human meals under any circumstances.

One reason for this is that certain foods are very harmful to your dog and can even be fatal. Another reason is that dog food should not be seasoned or spiced. If you observe these aspects, you can feed your Newfoundland cooked foods without concern.

Normally, dog food consists of the same components as human food, meat, vegetables and a satiating portion, except that the distribution of those components varies. Home-cooked foods for your dog would include:

- **Meat:**

  Beef, poultry, lamb and almost any other types of meat are suitable for dogs to eat. However, with pork you will need to ensure that it is cooked through. Offal is rich in vitamins and trace elements but should not be given too often.

- **Fish:**

  Almost all kinds of fish are suitable for your dog and he will love them too. Please be careful that you remove all bones or they would lead to the same problems as we humans have.

- **Eggs:**

  Eggs are high in protein and make for shiny fur. A small amount of the shells can also be used.

- **Milk/Dairy products:**

  Many dogs are intolerant to dairy products, there are only a few which are suitable. These include curd, sour milk and cottage cheese.

- **Grain:**
  Rice, oatmeal, pasta and bread are very well digested by most dogs and can be mixed in with the home-made feed.

- **Pulses:**
  These can only be fed cooked and if possible chopped, then they can be added to the feed.

- **Fruit/Vegetables:**
  Both fruit and vegetables are well liked by many dogs. The best way to add them to the feed is shredded or pureed.

At this point I would like to add that some foods which can be eaten by humans without problems are harmful to our four-legged friends and can even be fatal. A list of these poisonous foods can be found in Chapter 4 under "Poisonous and other problematic substances".

I personally use home-made food for two very different reasons. The first is that the food can be made very bland. If my beloved companion is suffering from a gastrointestinal problem, I would only give him bland foods for a couple of days, as I later describe. Since I am cooking his food, I can cater for what my dog's already weakened digestive system will be able to deal with.

In addition, I like to prepare snacks and treats myself. You can make them in large amounts in advance and use them as you need them.

The second reason I like to make my own dog food is so that I can pamper them. When I cook the food myself, I believe I am doing something which my dogs will enjoy. I have detailed the 10 recipes, which my dogs seem to like best, at the end of this book. I hope you will have as much enjoyment from trying them out as I do.

VEGETARIANISM AND VEGANISM

For staunch vegetarians and vegans, dealing with meat is not easy. For this reason, many people decide to feed their dogs vegetarian food (without meat) or even vegan food (purely plant-based). There is a lot of heated discussion as to whether this form of feeding is at all appropriate for dogs.

If owners decide to feed their dogs vegetarian food, this seldom has anything to do with the health of the dogs but is mostly based on ethical or religious grounds. For some owners, who build a close relationship with their animals, the thought of intensive animal farming or slaughter is simple unacceptable and is the reason why they want to give their dog a vegetarian diet.

The argument that this form of nutrition is not natural is weakened by the fact that this also goes for tinned foods. Even the Animal Protection Association PETA supports feeding vegetarian foods. In the meantime, there are countless studies, many in favour and just as many against it. As I already mentioned at the beginning of this book, dogs are not purely meat eaters but they eat many varied things, although their digestive systems are developed to deal predominantly with meat.

What can you do if you do not wish to feed your dog meat?

On the one hand, I would ask you to consider if you have chosen the right kind of pet for yourself. The question whether meat is necessary for your dog or not is not yet scientifically resolved. There are many animals which prefer vegetarian foods and eat them voluntarily and happily. I would recommend any staunch vegetarian not to choose a dog as a pet. I believe that a wholly plant-based diet does not cover the important amino acids that your dog needs on a regular basis.

However, should you be firmly of the opinion that you want to have a dog, I would recommend that you do this in consultation with a dog nutrition expert. It is your responsibility to ensure that he gets all the minerals, trace elements and vitamins he needs. Create a feeding plan with the expert and make sure that your Newfoundland's blood values are regularly checked.

I do not see any problem with occasionally feeding your dog only on plant-based foods. My dog, Daika, for example loves cucumber above everything and she often gets it as a snack. Sometimes, I leave out the meat component in the homemade meals, but not in all meals and certainly not the majority of the time.

As an alternative to vegetarian food and tinned food, you can buy your dog's feed from controlled, organic, non-laboratory tested animal sources, for use in the previously mentioned BARF or homecooked methods. Having all these alternatives means that you can rest assured that what your dog is eating is not the result of intensive farming or animal cruelty.

I am completely opposed to the sole feeding of vegetarian meals for dogs and I do not want to go into further detail about it here. I can only repeat my suggestion that, in future, owners choose another animal, rather than a Newfoundland as a pet.

WHAT YOU NEED TO CONSIDER WHEN FEEDING YOUR NEWFOUNDLAND

The good news to start with: Unlike other breeds, the Newfoundland does not demonstrate any breed-typical intolerances or deficits. For that reason, you do not need to concern yourself about anything in principle when feeding your dog, which cannot be said for some breeds.

Because of his size and genetic predisposition, this breed tends towards getting hip displacement. I will be speaking about this in a later chapter of this book. Also, false nutrition can cause this condition to escalate, for example when your Newfoundland is overweight.

But how can you, as a layperson, recognise if your Newfoundland is being fed correctly?

A healthy Newfoundland should have a flat, sinewy belly, and strong limbs, which do not have a fatty layer. His fur should shine, his eyes should be watchful and attentive and he should always be ready to move. Laziness is not normal behaviour for a Newfoundland and could be a sign of incorrect feeding.

Feeding Newfoundlands with BARF foods is particularly popular in comparison to other breeds. Many owners believe it is important to feed their dogs with breed-specific food and with fresh meat and people are more willing to do that because of their dog's origins as a working dog.

Naturally, you can feed him wet or dry foods without concern. Also here, it is important to ensure the quality and the origin of the food. If it covers the nutritional needs of your dog and if he tolerates it well, any type of food is suitable.

REGULATING YOUR NEWFOUNDLAND'S WATER SUPPLY

There has been much discussion about the right amount, quality and type of food for your dog, but there is something which he needs more urgently than food: Water!

If necessary, your dog could live for a long time without food if he had to, but he could only exist for a few days without water. On the following pages, you will discover how much water your Newfoundland needs and how you can convince him to drink, if he is not drinking enough.

REGULATING THE WATER REQUIREMENT OF YOUR NEWFOUNDLAND.

Your Newfoundland cannot live for long without sufficient water, as he needs it for many of his physiological functions. For example, he needs water to break down the components of food in his digestive system, in order to extract the nutrients into the bloodstream and then into the tissues where it can transport toxic substances out through the kidneys or regulate his body temperature.

You can see how many physiological processes are dependent upon drinking enough water. Normally, this can be achieved in three different ways:

1. **By actively drinking:** This is how your dog satisfies most of his water requirement and is the most obvious method.

2. **Through his food:** Even while eating, your dog can take in fluids. Naturally, there is a great difference depending on whether he is given wet or dry food. Dogs fed with BARF food can obtain most of their daily requirement through the fresh food.

3. **Through his metabolism:** As strange as it may seem, your dog is able to cover some of his water requirement through his metabolic processes.

It is important to keep your Newfoundland's water intake at a constant level in order that his physiological functions can work properly. It is not good if your dog can only quench his thirst once a day. It can cause deficiency symptoms and he will probably be very thirsty. In order to avoid that, you should ensure that he always has access to water.

The water you set down for him should always be clean and, if it is given in a bowl, I recommend cleaning it regularly – at least once a week – with dishwashing liquid or vinegar essence. Remember to rinse off remnants of your cleaning liquid carefully so that it does not enter his system. I suggest you take water with you when you exercise your Newfoundland. Of course, he can also drink from puddles and ponds, but water can easily be contaminated with germs, if it is standing. Some ponds are breeding grounds for bacteria. Your dog should be able to drink flowing water, which seems clean in most countries, without worries.

Tap water is quite safe to drink in Germany. However, if it is highly chlorinated, some dogs will refuse to drink it because of its taste. For a few weeks I would suggest giving him still mineral water. Fizzy water is not necessarily harmful for your dog but it could cause stomach problems and flatulence. Take care to give him his water at room temperature. If it is too cold, it can also cause irritation of the stomach, vomiting or diarrhoea. Alternatively, dogs often refuse to drink water which is too warm.

A healthy Newfoundland loses fluids through various ways during the day. It can be lost through his stools, in his urine, through his breath, skin and by lactating dogs, through the teats. Many factors dictate how much water your dog needs. These include his weight, how much fluid he has lost through the above-mentioned methods, the air temperature, the amount of physical activity he has had, or through his food. Three quarters of his requirement can be satisfied using wet food.

You can use this rule of thumb to give you an idea how much water your Newfoundland needs each day:

A fully-grown Newfoundland who is fed with dry food, at a normal air temperature of about 20°C, moving an average amount, needs about 40 to 100 ml of water per kilogram body weight. A dog of 65 kg would need 2,600 to 6,500 ml. If he is fed wet food, that amount reduces by about 20 to 50 ml per kilogram body weight. This would be 1,300 to 3,250 ml for an average-sized Newfoundland.

If your dog is exercising more or if the air temperature rises, the water requirement will increase accordingly. The same applies to particularly salty food. As with us humans, that can also lead to an increased requirement of water. I have given you the rule of thumb, but as you can see, there is a lot of leeway upwards and downwards. If he is drinking much more or less than that, you should consult with your dog's veterinary surgeon, as it could be sign of a disease of some kind.

If your Newfoundland is drinking roughly the amounts mentioned above, everything would seem to be alright. Once you have watched your dog's water intake for a few weeks, you will see how much he normally needs and how more exercise or higher temperature affects his thirst. As always, you should make adjustments according to the specific needs of your dog.

HOW TO ENCOURAGE YOUR NEWFOUNDLAND TO DRINK

Normally, a healthy dog will drink enough water, provided it is available to him, as dogs listen to their bodies carefully, which cannot be said for humans.

However, even a healthy dog may not drink enough. One reason could be the high temperatures in summer when your dog needs to drink more than he is used to. It could also be caused by a stress situation. As with us humans, a dog can also refuse to eat and drink when stressed. Particularly with male dogs, it can happen if they see a bitch on heat.

Here are a few tips from me to ensure that your dog is drinking enough:

- Give him more water than usual. You could exchange some of his dry food for wet food, which automatically increases his intake. You would not normally add water to wet food but, in this case, I would suggest you do.

- Give him water with flavour. Bouillon, liver sausage or sausage water are good examples, but ensure that the water is not too salty.
- Add fruit to the water, such as cranberries or bilberries. This way, you can make the drink more interesting and many dogs try to fish the fruit out of the water, just for fun. At the same time, they are automatically swallowing water.
- Think about buying a water dispenser. Some dogs drink much better if you give them running water to drink.

If your dog is still refusing to drink, or drinking less than would be considered normal, even after trying all the above, I suggest you consult your vet. It is possible that he has an illness that you need to check out.

On the following pages you will find a checklist which covers all the main points regarding the drinking behaviour of your Newfoundland.

Checklist of Drinking Behaviour:

- ☐ Always provide enough water for your Newfoundland.
- ☐ Ensure that the water is room temperature and is not sparkling so as to avoid problems with his stomach.
- ☐ Clean his water bowl regularly.
- ☐ Do not let him drink from still waters while he is out, take fresh water with you for your dog.
- ☐ Increase the amount of water you give him if he has been very active or if the outside temperatures are high.
- ☐ Add bouillon, liver sausage or sausage water to his drink, to awaken his interest.
- ☐ Soften dry food in plenty of water and optionally add some wet food to his meal.
- ☐ Add some fruit to the water to make a playful way of awakening his interest to drink.

- ☐ Consult a vet if, despite trying all of the above, your dog is still not drinking, appears tired and lacking in motivation.

- Chapter 3 -

BASICS OF GROOMING

We humans take for granted that we take care of our bodies. However, what is normal for us is not always true for our dogs. I would even go so far as to say that most dog owners assume that they do not need to take care of their dog's grooming, as he would do what is necessary himself.

In principle, this assumption is not completely wrong. However, certain breeds need much more care than others.

With your Newfoundland, you have chosen a breed which needs more grooming than a Pug, as an example. You must be clear from the beginning that you will regularly have to invest a significant amount of time on this aspect.

Taking care of his fur will belong to your daily routine and it is important that you get him used to checking over and taking care of his fur. You should start with it cautiously.

If your Newfoundland is not used to having his fur checked over and groomed, I suggest starting with it cautiously. Do not start straight away with the full programme that you will find in this book. It is better to begin with short periods of checking him over and repeating the process several times a day, so that he can get used to it. Try to make the examination and the grooming as pleasurable as possible for him and sweeten it with treats, strokes and praise if your Newfoundland stays still and behaves as you would like him to.

The most important thing is that you stay calm. Even if your dog is wriggling around, you need to stay calm and composed. If you react to his behaviour and become irritated or even angry, you will only achieve the opposite. The tension in your dog will only increase and he will begin to hate the examinations. This will set the tone for many years of stress and regular conflict. So, stay calm, no matter what your Newfoundland does!

Again, I recommend the following: Begin with small steps and do not overstress your Newfoundland. Every step, which is carried out confidently, is much more valuable than an over-hasty big step which is carried out with uncertainty.

I am often asked why it is necessary to make such a big thing about grooming, even though your dog descended from the wolf and that the wolf never had anyone looking after it. This argument seems sensible at first, but does not withstand closer examination.

In comparison to the wolf, which can reproduce freely, today's pet dogs are bred purposefully to show specific characteristics, which, according to Darwin's theory, would not have established themselves in the wild. Humans have influenced greatly how the various breeds have developed and how certain characteristics have been fostered, which need receive special attention. For example: The lop ears of a Newfoundland.

In addition, the life of a pet dog is vastly different from that of a wolf. Living with humans has made dogs dependent on us, which is most noticeable by the amount of care they need.

There are also simple aspects which come into play, such as being able to keep your home cleaner if you regularly brush your Newfoundland. Instead of him losing his long hair little by little, as happens with the wolf, brushing him will help to loosen his fur quicker and at the same time minimise the hair flying around in your home.

As I already mentioned, with your Newfoundland you have chosen a breed which needs more care than the average. Because of this, I have explained in the following pages how you can regularly check the eyes, skin, fur, ears, teeth and paws of your Newfoundland. If you stick to this regime, it will ensure that you are able to notice signs of sickness in the early stages and you and your dog will feel much better.

The tips on the following pages are based on the opinions of doctors, advisors and other experts. If you follow the procedure exactly, you will soon be spending many hours checking and grooming your dog. It is probable that you will suspect illness and danger everywhere with your four-legged friend at first – I do not want to burden you with that. Here, you will read about many problems which could affect your Newfoundland. However, it is important that you understand that the word "could" does not mean that problems "will" occur and certainly not all at once.

As with all things, it is important that you listen to your common sense. If your dog has already had problems with his eyes, you need to look after them more than you would with a dog which has always had healthy eyes. If your dog is showing no sign of abnormalities, do not wear him out with unnecessary inspections and special care programmes. Just do what is necessary correctly and leave anything which is not necessary.

At the end of each chapter, I will give a recommendation, based on what I consider to be necessary for my dogs and what I think can be ignored. Please do not follow my recommendations blindly but take care of the needs of your own dog in particular. Every dog is different and his needs are different, but with the help of my recommendations, I want to give you a feeling for the appropriate care which your dog needs specifically.

EYE CARE

The sweet, heart-warming look that your dog gives you is part of your relationship with him. In order to keep it that way, it is important that you inspect his eyes regularly. Experts and vets recommend checking your dog's eyes every day.

The eyes of a healthy dog should be clear and shiny. The eye lids should be close to his eye ball and be clean. There should be no mucus or incrustation. If your dog shows a dryness in his eyes just after waking up, that is quite normal and is similar the rheum or sleep dust which we humans often get in our eyes.

If you want to inspect his eyes, hold his head gently in your hands and, if necessary, stroke the hair to the side.

If you notice that your dog often has that rheum in his eyes, you could wipe his eyes gently every morning with a damp cloth to clean it away. Take care that the cloth you use is not fluffy or you could end up getting some in his eyes. You should use a separate cloth for each eye, so that any bacteria are not transferred from one eye to the other.

If your dog often has problems with his eyes, you could exchange the plain water on the cloth with a warm saline solution or camomile tea. The water to be used in any case should be filtered to ensure that there is no residue which can transfer to your dog's eye.

If your Newfoundland tends to have long hair around his eyes, it is a good idea to have it cut regularly. This way, no hair impurities will transfer into your dog's eyes and his hair itself will not irritate them.

The following symptoms could be a clue that there is something wrong with your dog's eyes and you should call the vet:

- Above average light sensitivity
- Touching his eyes with his paw
- Sensitivity to the touch
- Thick discharge coming from the eye
- Heavy, bloodshot eyes
- Enlarged pupils
- Any changes in the eye

In addition, I advise you to protect your dog from getting too much dust or pollen in his eyes. Even though the Newfoundland is not a small breed which is so close to the ground and that he would particularly suffer from that, you still need to be aware of the possibility.

Do not let him walk through flowery meadows or over very dusty fields. The small particles can get into his eyes very quickly and cause conjunctivitis. If you cannot avoid taking him to places with large amounts of pollen or dust, I suggest you rinse his eyes after his walk with a mild cleaning agent without additives. Such cleaning agents can be obtained from most drugstores or pet shops.

As well as pollen and dust, you should avoid dry air in the home. Just like we humans, a dog can suffer from dry, heated air, which can cause burning or runny eyes. However, unlike humans, the dogs do not know why and so do not avoid being close to fireplaces and heaters. If you notice that your Newfoundland dog often suffers from runny eyes or blinks often, particularly in the wintertime, it would be helpful to increase the humidity in the room. This will not only improve the symptoms in your dog's eyes, but also in your own.

Just as dogs do not recognise dry, heated air, they also do not recognise draughts. In fact, many dogs deliberately lie with their heads in the draught. Try to prevent your dog from doing that too often because it can also lead to conjunctivitis.

My recommendations for you:

If your dog is not suffering from problems with his eyes, you will not need to examine them specifically each day. Some dogs never need to have the discharge removed from their eyes. That does not mean that your dog does not have any, but that up to that point it has cleared up by itself. If I notice anything, I would keep my eye on it and, as long as it does not get any worse, I would not take any action.

The tips with the draught and dry, heated air need to be taken seriously. It does not take long to fix and it will save your dog a lot of suffering.

SKIN AND FUR CARE

Generally, a dog's fur is seen as the mirror to his health. If his fur is shiny, full and robust, you can assume that your Newfoundland is healthy. However, as soon as this changes and the fur becomes dull and brittle, or if it is excessively matted, or your dog is losing a lot of fur, there may be a problem. The problem could lie deeper – often fur problems can be caused by irritations. Other problems could be nutritional deficiencies or parasites.

The skin is not only your dog's largest organ, it also carries out some very important tasks:

- **It protects your dog from pathogens.** It serves as an immunological barrier and deters bacteria, fungi and other harmful substances from entering the inner organs.

- **It regulates the temperature of your dog.** By widening or tightening the blood vessels, it protects your dog from the heat or cold.

- **It supports your dog through communication.** Tiny muscles in the skin enable the fur to stand up on end. In addition, smells and hormones can be emitted through the skin.

- **It helps to detoxify.** Waste products from the metabolic processes and other harmful substances are discharged through the skin.

- **It is responsible for replenishing the fur.** The hair follicles which form the fur on your dog, are found in the skin. The skin replaces the fur twice a year.

To ensure that your dog has not only healthy skin but also beautiful fur, you need more than regular grooming; you need to give him a balanced diet. Many dog owners do not know that nutritional deficiencies first show themselves on the skin and fur.

You may be asking yourself what healthy skin looks like on your Newfoundland. Usually, your dog will present with white to grey-coloured skin.

If the skin is reddened, dry or scaly, or your dog seems to be scratching a lot, this could be a symptom of a skin disorder. The same can be said for dull or oily fur and hair loss.

Experts recommend grooming the skin and fur daily while at the same time carrying out your examination. It does not have to be a boring routine. It could become a cherished ritual which could strengthen your relationship with each other.

Daily brushing and massaging does take longer than with a pug, for example. However, if you remain on the ball, it will become less work as the amount of hair and skin particles which are shed as a result are less than if you were to do this routine less regularly Through daily brushing I also remove dirt particles remaining from his walks before they spread all over the house and I can also notice tics, fleas and other parasites much quicker.

If a Newfoundland is not used to daily brushing and reacts anxiously or even aggressively to it, I offer the same advice as with his eye care. Take it slowly and using a lot of treats and strokes. Try to make his daily brushing as pleasant an experience as possible so that he looks forward to it. Start with giving him a lot of attention before you reach for a soft brush. Wait until your dog is relaxed with that before you change to a harder brush or even to an undercoat brush. I always recommend brushing in the reverse direction – meaning from the tail to the head. After that you can brush from head to tail. Once your Newfoundland is well brushed, you can begin to go through his fur with the wide-tooth comb. After that, you can change to a fine-tooth comb. This regular procedure protects your Newfoundland's fur from matting. Once it is matted, in a lot of cases the only solution is to have it all cut off.

You are lucky that your Newfoundland, like his ancestor the wolf, has a full upper coat and thick undercoat. His fur is very robust, natural and apart from that needs little grooming – at least on the part of your dog as it does not bother him if there are dog hair everywhere in your home – you probably think differently about that.

You should not really bath your Newfoundland except to get rid of any dirt which you think necessary. Intensive bathing and particularly shampooing destroy the natural protection and oil layer of the fur and skin. This can lead to skin irritation and itchiness. Only bathe your dog in exceptional circumstances and only use shampoo if it is absolutely necessary.

Never use human shampoo as your Newfoundland has a different pH-value and therefore his skin does not react well to it. You can find dog shampoo in all normal pet shops.

In preparation for bathing, I suggest putting down a non-slip pad in the shower or bath tub. Make sure that the water is warm but never hot.

The first time you bathe him be very gentle and take it slowly. Shower your dog down very carefully, beginning with each individual paw. If your Newfoundland remains quiet and relaxed, then go on to shower his legs. Slowly work towards the front, starting with the tail, continuing down his flanks and back.

Only shower over his head when your dog is used to bathing or is completely relaxed. If he is not, I suggest using a damp cloth instead. Do not use the shampoo on his head to avoid soap getting into his eyes, ears, muzzle or nose. Be just as careful when hosing down with fresh water.

If your Newfoundland begins to panic, stop what you are doing straight away. He needs to feel good about it and you cannot achieve that with pressure. Try giving him treats and petting him to get him to relax. The main thing is that you remain calm and do not get angry, annoyed or show that you are stressed.

When you are finished with bathing, your Newfoundland will probably want to give himself a good shake. Try drying him as well as you can in the shower or bath tub. Do not rub too hard. Many dogs do not like the hairdryer. You can test it if you like but if your dog does not like it, then it is better to stop. In winter you need to ensure that the environment around your dog is warm until his thick undercoat is dry. In the summer, when it is warm, you can leave the towelling down and hair-drying completely as your dog will enjoy his cool, wet fur very much.

Care products, such as sprays can be used but are not really necessary. If your dog is receiving a balanced, nutritional diet, his fur will shine without using them.

You do not need to plan regular visits to the grooming salon with your Newfoundland. In contrast to other breeds, he does not need to be trimmed or cut. However, if you put a lot of value on the optics of your dog, I recommend choosing your grooming salon well, as there are black sheep in this industry too. Make sure he prepares your dog slowly for the procedure and does not overstress him.

My recommendation for you:

I do not undertake a special inspection of his fur or skin as this is not necessary. We have a tradition at home that our dogs get a lot of petting in the evenings. I use this time to have a closer look at their fur.

I am quite flexible with brushing. In principle I brush my beloved dogs once a weekevery second day. While I am doing that, I look closely at the places which are difficult to access, such as behind the ears, or elbows, where matting can often occur. Apart from that, my Newfoundland's fur more or less cleans itself. However, if he is beginning to moult, I brush him every day. I also brush him thoroughly after a long, rainy walk when his fur is very dirty. I usually wait until he is dry before I brush him, to get the dirt out of his fur, so that I do not have to bathe him. Sometimes I do not get all the dirt out the first time, so the next day I repeat the brushing - several times if necessary.

If your dog has acute or chronic problems with his skin, or his fur, this procedure may suit you.

EAR CARE

I do not need to stress how important the ears are for your Newfoundland. They serve not only for him to hear, but are important for his balance and communication with his fellow creatures. Regular, daily inspection of the ears is therefore recommended by experts.

The dog's ear consists of three parts:

- The outer ear
- The middle ear
- The inner ear

He can hear much better than you or I and recognises additional frequencies which are higher or lower than those which we can hear. In order to keep it that way, you need to inspect your dog's ears regularly.

Ideally, you will not find anything, because a healthy dog's ear is well supplied with blood and clean. Your dog's body is able to produce its own cleaning mechanisms. For example, it is able to produce enough wax to get rid of impurities, fine protective hair prevents dust particles and other such foreign bodies from entering the inner ear, and good ventilation prevents bacteria from multiplying in the warm, damp climate.

The most common problem in dogs' ears affects the outer ear and outer ear canal. The following symptoms could mean that something is not quite right:

- There is a strange, unpleasant smell coming out of his ear.
- His ear passage is very dirty or sticky (e.g. a black substance or ear wax).
- You notice small black spots in his ear (it could be parasites).
- His ear is red or even discharging (be careful, this could be an infection).
- You see a fresh wound or bleeding of some kind.
- You notice that your Newfoundland is often scratching his ears, or shaking his head, or perhaps not holding his head straight.

I would suggest calling a vet if any of these symptoms appear. However, if his outer ear is only slightly soiled, you can try to clean it yourself.

Use a damp, fuzz-free cloth, which you can wrap around your index finger and carefully clean the ear shell. It is important not to wet the cloth too much and that no moisture gets into his middle ear. Make sure to dry his outer ear well, as the moisture can cause the bacteria to multiply around the area. If you prefer, you can use camomile tea instead of water as this also acts as an anti-inflammation agent. Ensure that the liquid you use is at room temperature.

If the ear is badly soiled, you can get a cleaning agent and drops from a specialist shop. I suggest applying it outside as your dog will want to shake his head violently afterwards. If the symptoms do not improve, you should consider taking your dog to the vet.

Under no circumstances should you use ear cotton swabs to clean his ears. The danger of pushing germs, wax or other dirt further into the ear is very great and you could cause bad injuries. In addition, if your dog makes a sudden movement, it could result in his eardrum being irreparably damaged.

Finally, I want to mention: Similar to the eye and skin care, I recommend getting your dog used to his ear care very early on in his life. Start slowly and carefully and link the examination and possible cleaning of his ears with lots of petting and one or two treats right from the beginning.

My recommendation for you:

As your Newfoundland does not have standing ears like a German Shepherd for example, he is more prone to having ear problems. I have a look at my dogs' ears every evening during cuddle time. That way I can see early on if there is any soiling to worry about. Up to now I have had very few problems with the ears of my dogs.

TOOTH CARE

We humans take care of our teeth as a matter of course, but many owners do not think it is necessary to do the same for their dogs. That is wrong. Your dog's teeth are used for communication, as a hunting weapon and as an eating tool. For these reasons it is important that they remain in good condition. You will find out how to do that in this chapter.

Just like us, your Newfoundland first cuts his milk teeth. These fall out after the third to sixth month, which sometimes leads to your puppy chewing everything in sight. He does that, by the way, to speed up the painful process of transitioning from baby to permanent teeth. An adult dog possesses 42 teeth which he needs to grab, hold onto, tear, kill and eat.

Get your dog used to you examining his teeth and gums on a regular basis. If you notice that the teeth are slightly discoloured yellow-brown or the gums have brown edges, you should see that as an alarm signal. It is probably plaque or a bacterial infection. If, in addition, your dog has an unpleasant smell on his breath, this is also a strong sign that he has tooth problems or gum inflammation. You may also notice bloody or very red-looking gums.

I strongly recommend not waiting until these symptoms occur but being proactive in providing good toothcare to reduce the chances of that happening. Statistically, 85% of all dogs over three years old suffer from tooth problems – a stunningly high number – which proves how important prevention is.

The main cause of plaque is being given the wrong food or leftovers, which stick between the teeth, causing bacteria to collect. The minerals in the saliva will turn the plaque into tartar which only the vet can get rid of.

Tooth care for your dog always begins with the food. Dogs which are only given softened dry food or wet food never have to chew. They swallow the small, soft pieces whole. Dogs which are given fresh, lean meat have to chew a lot more and that is exactly where natural tooth care begins.

Chewing automatically cleans the surface of your Newfoundland's teeth and avoids plaque and later tartar to form. The increased saliva flow while chewing will assist in the cleaning. This is even more effective when your dog is given bones as well as meat. However, it is important that the bone is always fresh (i.e. not cooked) and not pork or chicken. In addition, it should be big enough that he cannot swallow it in one go, which is particularly important with puppies.

Chew toys or other special chewing items from the pet shop are a good substitute for the natural tooth care. There is also the possibility of giving your Newfoundland a thorough tooth clean with special dog toothbrushes and toothpaste.

Did you know that active dogs have significantly less problems with their teeth? Scientific studies have shown that dogs produce more saliva during sporting activities, which helps the tooth-cleaning process.

My recommendation for you:

I personally recommend only physically cleaning your dog's teeth if he has had problems with them in the past or if specific genetic characteristics are present.

It should be sufficient to give your Newfoundland chewing items or bones if he is healthy. Ensure that your dog is only given unsugared food. Feeding too many treats in between meals can also increase plaque formation.

If your dog is not suffering from illness, you do not need to look at your dog's teeth and gums every day. Once a week should be enough. If your dog is refusing his food, or has a strong mouth odour, I suggest taking a look at his teeth. Sometimes that can be the reason.

Just like us humans, the same applies to dogs: The older the dog, the more vulnerable the teeth and gums will become. You will probably not find any abnormalities or notice any disorders in a young, healthy dog during the first few years. The older your Newfoundland becomes, the more probable it will be that he will develop plaque. For this reason, you will need to adjust your inspection frequencies to his age.

PAW CARE

Many people think that pedicures for dogs are extravagant – but I and many experts see it differently.

Perhaps you have noticed that your Newfoundland has been licking his paws or chewing on his claws. If he has, he urgently needs a pedicure. It is not strictly a cosmetic treatment as it is also important care which can prevent serious health problems.

But why is it necessary at all? After all, the wolf even nowadays does not need a pedicure as nature takes care of his important paw care. For the most part, the wolf walks over hard ground, rocks and stones from being a puppy, causing the claws and hair on his paws to be rubbed off regularly.

It is different with modern dogs. They walk mostly on soft ground and are only out in their natural surroundings for a few hours per day. Life with us humans has caused additional burdens on our dogs which were unknown to the wolf, such as de-icing salt.

How do you know if your Newfoundland needs some paw care?

- If his claws touch the ground (your dog's feet make clicking noises when he walks over tiles).
- If your dog is licking or chewing on his feet.
- If your dog stumbles a lot
- If your dog sets his paws at an unusual angle while walking

If you notice any of these signs, you should take a closer look at your dog's paws. In addition, many experts recommend inspecting the paws at least once a week or after a long walk.

Look closely if dirt has become lodged between the pads or under the claws. If so, you should remove it. If the hair between the pads is so long that it protrudes out of them, you should cut it shorter. Dirt and small stones can gather in the hair which can become painful. Also, the hair can become matted, with the result that your dog has less grip, particularly on slippery surfaces, and can slip and stumble. I suggest buying a pair of special scissors with rounded ends. If the paws are badly soiled, a lukewarm footbath could help.

If you notice cracks, cuts or even in-growing claws, you should consult your vet. You can use an oily cream or

Vaseline (particularly with cracked pads) but I suggest getting them looked at by your vet, particularly if the problem continues over a longer period of time or happens often. In both cases, using camomile in the footbath can be quite effective.

In the winter, your dog's paws need particular care. Grit, ice and salt can place a lot of strain on them. During the cold months, you should try to avoid gritted roads as much as you can and check his paws after every walk. I put Vaseline on my dogs' feet after each walk. If your dog is already suffering from wounds and split pads in the warmer months, you could think about buying special dog shoes for him. You will need to make sure that they fit well, are of good quality and also that your dog can not take them off by himself.

Now we come to claw care: If the claws are too long, your Newfoundland is not able to walk putting his pads down first but steps directly onto his claws (which is what causes the clicking sound). During the rolling motion, the claws are pushed into the claw bed which can cause painful pressure on the pads. If the pressure becomes too strong, your dog will try to avoid this by putting his paw down on the side. In turn, this can lead to long-term muscle hardening, joint damage and deformity of his musculoskeletal system.

If you are not sure if your dog's claws are too long, try the following: Let your Newfoundland stand in front of you. Make sure that his weight is evenly distributed on all four paws. Try sliding a piece of paper under the claws towards the pads. If you are not able to do that, his claws are too long, they should be about 2mm above the ground.

Clipping claws can really be done by anyone. However, I suggest that you let your vet show you how to do it the first time, as there is a part of the claw which contained nerves and blood vessels, which we call the "quick". You should never cut into the quick because that is very painful for your dog and the claw can bleed profusely.

Never rely on the spacer on your claw clippers when deciding how far to clip, you should always monitor it yourself. I suggest staying well away from the quick. If you look carefully, you can usually see where the quick starts. Sometimes it is useful to use a torch under the claw to be able to see it better.

It is very important that your dog is lying quietly while you are clipping his claws so that he does not suddenly try to pull his foot away. I always try to tire out my Newfoundland before I start because that increases the chances of him staying still. Do not hold the paw too loosely. Remember though, that you want to make his claw clip as pleasant as possible. Use a lot of treats and strokes here.

Only cut the horny part of the claw with the clippers. You should stop before you reach the part which is not hardened. Hold the clippers horizontally and ensure that you clip at a right angle to the claw's growth direction. Do not cut any more than a few millimetres at a time, so that you do not cut too much. Do not forget the so-called wolf's claw at the end. That is the fifth claw on the back leg which is rounded in appearance and does not touch the ground, but it has to be clipped.

Stay calm during the procedure and keep him well grounded. Do not overtax him and praise him well once you are finished.

You also need to remain calm if you happen to damage the quick. It will look worse than it is because of the heavy bleeding. Hold a gauze pad or compress against the injury and wait for a few minutes. Normally, the bleeding will have stopped by then. If it has not, you can try an old household remedy by mixing some flour and water to a thick mass. Place the mass onto a gauze pad and press onto the wound again for a few minutes. The mass will form a clump and act as a kind of plug on the wound.

If the bleeding has not stopped after about 20 minutes, you should call your vet. If it has stopped, it would be best to lightly bandage the wound and then put a clean, old sock over the hole paw. You can stick it into place with sticky tape so that your Newfoundland does cannot bite or pull it off. The sock should ensure that the fresh wound does not become soiled and you should keep it on for about a week. Check it daily to ensure that it does not become infected. If your dog behaves normally, in my opinion it is probably not necessary to call a vet.

If you want to file the claw after you have cut it, so that there are no sharp edges, you should ensure that you are only filing in one direction. If you file backwards and forwards, this could cause your Newfoundland some pain. In addition, it is not good for the structure of his claw – by the way, the same applies to finger nails.

As I said before, looking after your dog's claws is not difficult but you need to be watchful, have a sure hand and lots of patience. As it is difficult for a beginner to know where the quick begins, it is a good idea to ask a professional – such as your vet – to show you. If you feel able to, you can do it from then onwards.

My recommendation for you:

I tend not to check my dog's paws very often except during the winter months. The salt, road grit and ice can often cause cracks in them, which I treat with Vaseline. My four-legged friends also have to wear the previously mentioned dog shoes from time to time, if necessary.

I do not need to check the length of my dogs' claws because I can hear when they get too long. Since I accidentally injured one of my dog's claws during clipping, I prefer to let the vet do it.

WHAT YOU NEED TO PAY PARTICULAR ATTENTION TO WITH YOUR NEWFOUNDLAND

As I mentioned at the beginning of this chapter, you have less things to worry about with your Newfoundland, as he is a really low maintenance breed compared to many others.

He was bred as a working dog who needed to find practical solutions. Because of this it was necessary to breed into him so that he would not need much grooming.

During the warm, summer months you should ensure that he always has enough fresh water and cool shade. His thick fur means that he does not cope with hot weather very well. Physical exertion should be left to the cooler morning hours.

In order to promote and maintain the well-being and health of your Newfoundland, I urge you not to forego the routine examinations which I have mentioned previously. Of course, there are many Newfoundlands who life long and happy lives without any of the care mentioned above. However, there are still many who suffer silently and no one notices their suffering. In the interest of your dog's well-being, you should invest the little time it takes in taking care of him.

The good part is: Not only the health of your Newfoundland will be increased, but also your relationship with him. Through intensive care a high level of trust will develop between you and your relationship with your dog will become even closer.

CHECKLIST: REGULAR CARE

- ☐ The eyes are clear and shiny. They are not reddened, there is no mucus or other changes.
- ☐ The skin is white to grey, not reddened, not dry or flaky.
- ☐ The fur is shiny and dense. There is no hair loss except for normal moulting.
- ☐ The ears are not dirty, nor showing signs of redness or dark spots and your dog is not shaking his head often or scratching his ears.
- ☐ The teeth are not showing a yellow-brown coating and the gums are not reddened or bleeding. There is no unpleasant breath.
- ☐ The paws are not cracked or sore, nor is there any distinguishable dirt between the pads.
- ☐ The claws are not touching the ground when your Newfoundland is standing normally.

CHECKLIST: CARE UTENSILS

- ☐ Claw clippers
- ☐ Tick tweezers
- ☐ Dog shampoo
- ☐ Brush (curry comb if necessary)
- ☐ Comb (coarse and fine-toothed, perhaps also a flea comb)
- ☐ Lotion or drops for cleaning the ears
- ☐ Fuzz-free cloths
- ☐ Camomile tea
- ☐ Chewing items (e.g. Chew toys or fresh beef bones)

- Chapter 4 -

COMMON ILLNESSES

For some owners, the health of their dog is almost more important than their own health. If the dog is not feeling well, neither is the person.

Luckily, we are living in times when we have a good health system for our animals. There are sufficient medicines, good vets and even clinics where our four-legged friends can receive excellent treatment.

Just like we humans, our dogs can suffer from all kinds of illnesses. Some of them are easy to treat, some are less easy. In some cases, we owners are able to help and in others there is no other choice but to visit the animal clinic.

In this chapter I will give you a brief summary of the most common illnesses, which can be caused by parasites and the gastro-intestinal conditions which occur most often. I will give you tips as to how to recognise them and what to do. At this point, it is important for me to emphasise that any serious conditions need to be treated by your vet. All these tips which I am listing below are meant for mild conditions.

In addition, I will give you a lot of helpful information on fever, vaccinations and castrating your Newfoundland, as well as those conditions which are typical for specific breeds.

The chapter ends with two checklists as to how you can recognise a healthy dog and what you need to have in your first-aid kit.

PARASITE INFESTATION

Many owners fear parasite infestations and not without good reason. These little insects can cause a lot of harm to our four-legged friends and some can also be transmitted to humans.

For this reason, I am outlining the three most common parasites – mites, ticks and fleas – in greater detail. You will discover how they get there, what they do and what you can do to get rid of them.

As with all parasites, it is important to detect them early on, then you can avoid greater harm. If you discover them late – meaning there is already a heavy infestation – it is much more difficult to remove them.

The best way to detect them early on is to follow the care inspection tips which I gave you in the previous chapter. Inspect your dog's fur regularly, particularly after a long walk on meadows and fields, then you will probably detect them early, which is the aim of the exercise.

In addition, there are a few things you can do to prevent infestation in the first place, but I will tell you that later in the individual sub-paragraphs in this chapter.

MITES

Mites belong to the spider family, but because of their size they are often only recognisable under a microscope. There are basically three types of mite, which differ by their mouth parts.

Chewing mites are at home in the ear passages of your dog and mainly feed on skin flakes. They cause skin infections and itchiness. Scratching, in turn, causes increased irritation which can lead to secondary infections and wounds.

Sucking mites have a trunk-like mouth with which they can suck blood and the lymphatic liquids of their host. This causes the danger of pathogens transferring to the host.

The last type is the *digging mite*. These "dig" through the outer skin layer, causing strong irritation which may lead to your dog injuring himself. In dogs we speak of "mange", in humans we say "scabies".

Probably the biggest danger facing your Newfoundland is the so-called grass mite, which belongs to the blood-sucking mite group. As the name suggests, these mites lurk in the grass, waiting for passing hosts.

Grass mites are only 0.3 millimetres in size and can be seen well because of their orange-coloured bodies. If you notice these creatures in your lawn at home, you can put out a white or light cloth on your grass during the summer. After a very short while, there will be a lot of orange spots collecting on the cloth to take a sunbathe.

They mostly attack places where they come directly in contact with your dog, such as the paws (often between the pads), the head (mostly on the bridge of the nose), the ears, the belly and the chest. They try to break into small cracks in the thinner parts of the skin and inject their saliva.

It is that saliva which causes intense irritation and, in some cases, a so-called mite allergy. The grass mites are not interested in your dog's blood but in the lymphatic fluid. You can see the affected areas because there is an orange colouring on the skin. In addition, if you go through his coat with a flea comb, you would probably notice small red spots in the fur. If not, then tap the comb onto a white cloth, where they will be more visible.

Unfortunately, there is no reliable preventative treatment against the attack of mites. There are some combi-treatments which are supposed to work against fleas, ticks and mites, but their success is dubious and questioned by many experts.

However, you are not completely helpless against them. There are a few things which you can do:

- Inspect your grass at home. If you can see grass mites, mow your lawn with greater frequency and treat it with stinging nettle compound. This successfully kills the larvae. It is important that you do not leave the cut grass on the lawn but remove it quickly.
- Examine your dog regularly after he has been playing in the meadows. The sooner you notice mite infestation, the better. If you do notice something, comb him thoroughly with a flea comb and give him a full bath. I suggest using an unscented ivory soap mixture, or in particularly acute cases, a mixture of olive oil, apple vinegar and salt water together with a mild, alcohol-based solution. Ensure that you only use lukewarm water and that you rinse your Newfoundland thoroughly afterwards.

Both of these suggested remedies will work against the skin irritation.

- Clean the floors of your home thoroughly too, and wash all the dog blankets. Vacuum other areas where you dog may have lain, such as the sofa.
- If your dog often suffers from heavy mite infestation, you should ask your vet for his advice on which suitable (chemical) product it would be best to use.

TICKS

As soon as the winter has passed and it starts to get warm, that is the time that the ticks get busy. Ticks also belong to the sucking group of the spider family as you had probably guessed. But contrary to grass mites, which are interested in the lymphatic liquids of their hosts, ticks are only interested in blood.

At the beginning, ticks are only as big as the head of a pin and can be difficult to spot or feel. But once they have found a host, and have nourished themselves on his blood for several days, the females in particular can grow up to 3 cm in size.

Ticks are mostly found on the edges of forests, in clearings, in grassland or parks. They climb on to high blades of grass or bushes and wait for their next victim. They have a particularly good sense of smell which helps them to prepare for the arrival of their host, i.e. they perceive the smell of sweat. They are also acutely aware of vibrations and changes in the CO2 content of the air. Once the tick has sensed a victim, it falls onto them and searches for a suitable place. Suitable places are mostly on thin-skinned areas but those well-circulating with blood, such as the head, haunches, ears or belly.

Most ticks prefer a particular kind of host. This is because they have usually specialised themselves on a particular host type by assimilating the anaesthetic part of their saliva secretion to them.

About 20 of the 900 tick species known world-wide, can be found in Germany. Your dog will probably only be attacked by three of them: The wood tick, the alluvial forest tick and the brown dog tick.

The fear that many people have for the tick is justified, as there are no other parasites which can transmit as many diseases. Ticks transmit bacteria in their saliva which can, for example, cause Borrelioses and other viruses which fall into the category of early-summer meningoencephalitis (ESME). It can also carry other parasites such as the Babesiosis which transmit toxins.

Not all such diseases are fatal but they can severely affect the health of your dog. For this reason, it is important to try and avoid tick bites and if your dog does get one, to recognise it quickly and remove it safely.

But what happens exactly when a tick bites?

Once it has found a suitable place, it cuts a slit in the skin of your dog with its mouthpiece and sticks its proboscis into the wound. Then it sucks the blood of its victim and at the same time introduces an anaesthetic into the wound, so that the dog does not notice that he is being bitten. The secretion also acts as an anti-inflammatory agent which blocks the immune system of the host, thereby preventing the wound from closing and enabling the blood flow to continue.

During its meal, the tick excretes the undigested blood through its bowel into the wound of its host, which is what causes the previously mentioned transfer of pathogens.

Unfortunately, there are no vaccinations which work against some of these diseases, so you just need to prevent them as best you can, using the measures which are available to you.

One of the most proven remedies is the tick collar. The best-known of these include the Scalibor collar, which has the active ingredient Deltamethrin and the Preventic collar which contains Amitraz. Both collars are neurotoxic and work by continually emitting the active substance through the fat layer of the skin. It takes about a week to get the full benefit but it lasts for between four and six months.

The main advantage of these collars is that the toxic effect is released slowly into your dog and is therefore gentler on his body. If your dog is intolerant to the ingredients or the collar causes side effects, you can remove it immediately. You should also take off the collar when he goes swimming as the active substance can harm aquatic animals.

Spot-on substances, that you dab onto the neck of your dog, work much quicker. These also remain effective for up to four months. The disadvantage of these is that your dog is subject to the whole toxic effect of the preparation at once. If your dog proves to be intolerant towards it or if it causes side-effects, there is little you can do about it.

Both solutions involve using nerve agents so you must decide for yourself if you want to give your dog any of these toxins. In addition, when you stroke your dog, you will also come into contact with these toxins to a lesser extent. Therefore, you need to be careful with their use, particularly if a cat lives in the same house as your Newfoundland, because they can be very poisonous for your feline pet. Be sure to read the instructions on the packet carefully or speak to your vet about it before you use anything – something which I would advise every owner to do.

The very popular amber collar is harmless for both your dog and the ticks. It is not scientifically proven that they work.

Another popular household remedy is garlic, which is rubbed into the dog. This, as well as other remedies such as essential oils, lavender and lemons is also ineffective.

Bogacare seems to be a promising natural remedy, which can be used on a collar or as a spot-on compound. However, tests are still in the early stages here.

If your dog should get bitten by a tick, despite all your efforts, it is important to remove the tick immediately. It does not matter whether you use a tick tweezer, card or lasso or normal household tweezers. Use the tool with which you feel most comfortable as all of them work equally well.

I personally prefer the tick tweezers and I describe below how best to get rid of ticks with them.

- Firstly, make a space around the tick by pushing the fur around the area to the side.

- Place the tweezers (or whatever you are using) as close to the skin as possible and surround the tick.

- Pull the tick out quickly, but whatever you do, do not pull it out with a jerk. Ticks do not have a screw thread, so there is no need to twist it while pulling it out.

- The best result is when you are able to remove its biting apparatus intact. If not, there is no need to panic. Do not try to remove it another way as you could cause more harm than good. Leave it in, after a while it will fall out by itself.

- Destroy the tick by burning, squashing (I recommend doing that outside the house between tissues) or dissolving it in alcohol. You should never put it into your household rubbish alive or flush it down the toilet, as ticks are very hardy little insects.

- **No-Go:** Never use other aids, such as nail polish remover, alcohol, oil, fire or glue. If you pour and of those onto the tick, you will cause it unnecessary stress, which could cause it to vomit into the wound and release even more pathogens into your dog's blood stream. In addition, you could injure your dog, particularly if you use fire.

Finally, I want to emphasise that the best agent against sicknesses caused by tick bites is regular inspection of the fur. There are no preparations presently on the market that I could recommend, as all of them have side effects or they are not proven effective. The earlier you discover the tick, the less time it has to introduce pathogens into your dog's body. Not every tick bite causes sickness. Only 0.1 – 5% of ticks carry the ESME-Virus within them.

But what can you do if your dog gets sick? If your Newfoundland starts to show symptoms after a tick bite, such as fever, fatigue or vomiting, you should contact your vet immediately. These symptoms could appear up to three weeks after the bite as the incubation period can last that long. Only your vet can confirm whether or not it is a sickness which has come from a tick bite. In order to give your vet the most accurate information, make a note of when you noticed and removed the tick. I usually also take a photo of it, so that the vet can see which kind of tick it is and is able to exclude a few sicknesses from the outset.

You should also check for a few weeks after that if the bite has healed properly. In most cases, I can say that such a bite heals without problems or consequences. Make sure that you do not panic. Stay calm and be careful while removing the tick.

FLEAS

Fleas also belong to the insect family and are true survivors. Their natural habitat is meadows and bushes, but they like to live in homes too and can live there all year long. Just like ticks and mites, the fleas wait for hosts and then jump onto them as they pass by. Even though they are only 3 millimetres long, they can jump up to 1 metre away and reach a height of 25 centimetres – a great distance for such a small creature.

There are thousands of different types of fleas in the world, but the German pet dog is mostly only sought by one particular type: the cat flea, whose favourite hosts are dogs and cats. However, if either of those do not happen to be available, they are quite happy to attach themselves to humans.

Contrary to popular belief, flea infestation has nothing to do with bad hygiene. Most pet dogs become infected through contact with other dogs or wild animals, such as hedgehogs, and bring them home where they usually breed rapidly. A female flea usually starts to lay eggs directly after its first blood meal and can continue to lay up to 50 eggs per day. The eggs fall out of the dog's fur and lie on the grass, carpet or other household textiles until they hatch about a week later. The larvae crawl into small cracks and after about 10 days are ready to find themselves a new host. In that time, a single flea could have laid up to about 850 more eggs.

The most important thing about flea infestation is that you catch it early so that you do not have a real invasion of fleas in the house. But how do you recognise a flea infestation?

The first sign is of course when you see an increase in your dog scratching himself as the flea's saliva causes a strong itch. Some dogs start to bite themselves, which often causes injury. Not every dog scratches himself enough to be noticed. There may be very little itchiness if it is only a light infestation, but in the meantime, masses of eggs will be falling onto the carpet, the sofa, your cushions and many other places in your home.

I have taken to checking for fleas during my daily fur examination. In addition to normal brushing, I always have a flea comb ready which has very fine, close teeth, with which I comb against the direction of growth. Then I shake the comb onto a piece of moist kitchen roll and take a good look at what is there. If I see small black-brown spots, I squeeze them carefully. If they turn rust brown to red, then it is likely to be flea excrement (digested blood). If the spots do not turn reddish, it is probably just normal dirt.

I do this test on a few different places and that way I can get a good picture of whether or not my dogs have fleas.

If this test indicates that your dog has an infestation, you need to act quickly as it can be said that only 5% of the fleas are actually on your dog. The other 95% are to be found as fleas, larvae or eggs in the surrounding area. For this reason, it is essential that the whole region around your dog be treated. Larvae can live for up to 6 months, without nourishment, in a crease in the sofa and are only waiting to find another host to jump onto.

Because only a fraction of the infestation is found on your dog, it is important not to rely solely on flea collars or spot-on preparations. They will only serve to ensure that the fleas want to escape from your dog and find a safer place to wait until the coast is clear. In the worst case, they could decide to choose you as a substitute host.

I do not need to tell you that this is not a good situation. But how can you challenge flea infestation successfully? I suggest following these three steps:

1. **Kill the fleas on your Newfoundland**

   Contact your vet immediately and ask him which agent is best to fight the infestation. On the one hand you need an insecticide (mostly in the form of a shampoo, spray or powder), which kills the fleas. As this agent alone will not kill all the fleas, you also need an inhibitor to prevent their development. To ensure that both compounds work at optimum levels you will need to repeat the process at specific intervals. You should discuss exactly what dosage and at what intervals with your vet as these preparations are poisonous. If necessary, you should also treat other animals who live in the household with you. Be aware that tick preparations and some flea preparations can be fatal to cats. Your vet will know exactly what is needed and will give you the right advice.

2. **Eliminate the flea brood in the area**

Once you have treated the fleas on your dog, you should start attacking the fleas, eggs and larvae in the area which your dog frequents.

Wash all floors daily (including the corners) with a wet mop and vacuum all carpets, upholstery and other furniture. Get rid of the dust bag immediately. You can smother it with anti-flea powder if you wish.

Wash all dog blankets, throws, cushions and covers at least at 60°C. You could use a chemical cleaner in addition to that (for example on sofa covers or carpets). Remember to clean your dog's stuffed animals too.

Wash all textiles at a minimum of 60°C.

Treat all surfaces where your dog lies and spray his blankets etc. with a special anti-flea powder or an environmental spray. Please take the advice of your vet about which to use and find out about the use of a so-called fogger which is a room spray which can kill fleas, eggs and larvae.

Remember to clean garages, cupboards, cars thoroughly and any other places where your dog may have recently been.

Even though it may seem difficult, if not impossible, you will need to keep this up for at least three months so that you can be sure you have caught all the eggs and larvae. If not, you have pre-programmed the next flea infestation.

3. **Take preventive action**

In addition to dealing with the fleas I would also recommend using a special anti-parasitic formula to ensure that all the extra work and costs in fighting the fleas is worth it. Ask your vet which remedy is most suitable for your dog. I personally prefer repelling anti-parasitic agents which prevent the flea from biting in the first place. However, as this is a poisonous pesticide, you should check with your vet that it will work quickly but gently on your Newfoundland.

In all the years I have been living together with dogs I have never had a flea infestation and I am very grateful for that. However, I know from those who have been through it how exhausting it can be for both humans and animals. Everyone I have spoken to who has suffered from a recurrence of the infestation, said that they did not adhere 100% to the recommended measures. I can only advise: If you happen to get fleas into the house, grit your teeth and hold out for the full three months, otherwise you will end up having the same problem again within a very short time.

GASTRO-INTESTINAL DISORDERS

Just like we humans, your dog can suffer from gastro-intestinal disorders. In this chapter I will describe the four most common gastro-intestinal problems which can be found in pet dogs.

Some owners are not always aware that they put their dogs into a danger which is quite avoidable, and I would like to change that. Sometimes it is the small things which you can do which can ensure that your Newfoundland is able to live a healthier life.

I will explain exactly what those things are on the following pages.

GASTRIC DILATATION VOLVULUS

Twisted stomach is one of the most-feared sicknesses which dogs can suffer from. If untreated (in this case that means unoperated), it can lead very quickly to the death of your dog.

Most dog owners have heard of it, but few know what causes it, how to recognise it and what to do about it.

It is mostly large breeds who suffer from twisted stomach, to which group the Newfoundland belongs. However, smaller breeds can also be affected. Apart from that, older dogs and in particular male dogs, are most prone to getting it.

As the name suggests, gastric torsion occurs when the stomach makes a complete turn inside the body, completely closing up the bowel entrance, oesophagus and blood vessels. If this occurs, there are no first aid methods which you can use to help your dog. The only thing which will help him is to get hold of a vet, or even better, an animal clinic, as quickly as possible so that he can have an operation to resolve it. The sooner the better.

If you see the following symptoms in your Newfoundland, you should act immediately.

- Your dog has a bloated stomach. In later stages it can even look like a drum.

- Your dog is very agitated.

- He refuses his food.

- His saliva production increases.

- He tries to vomit but without success.

Luckily there are a few ways to prevent twisted stomach. Here are a few examples:

- Divide his daily ration into several smaller portions rather than giving it all to him at once.

- Avoid allowing him to play and frolic directly after he has eaten. Your dog should remain quiet for at least 30 minutes after his meal.

If you stick to these two tips, there is little probability that your Newfoundland will ever suffer from a twisted stomach.

DIARRHOEA

Diarrhoea in dogs, much as in humans, is when there is an increased frequency of bowel movement where the consistency is mostly soft to runny.

It is a very unspecific symptom of any illness as it often happens with a variation of conditions, ranging from harmless to serious. In most cases, however, it is more harmless and disappears within a few days.

The reasons for this could be simply that your dog ate too fast or too much, so that his stomach could not tolerate it, or if he has a sensitive nature, he may have reacted sensitively towards stress, excitement or some changes in living conditions.

The biggest danger with diarrhoea is dehydration, so you should ensure that his water bowl is always filled. As a second step, I suggest that you make him fast for a day (at least 24 hours), really giving him nothing to eat, not even a treat! This will give your dog time for his intestines to recover. On the following day, start by giving him a small portion of light food. A good example of this could be boiled rice with cooked chicken (important: without bones!) and cottage cheese. Most dogs love it, but if your dog is not so keen, you could add some vegetables or broth to the rice for some taste, but not so much broth as it could be too spicy for him.

You can increase the portions on the following days and when his condition has improved, you can go back to his normal food, step by step by reducing the amount of light food and increasing the amount of his normal food.

If the diarrhoea has not improved after two days, or is mixed with blood, you should contact your vet, particularly if he is showing other symptoms, such as vomiting and fever. Puppies are in increased danger, because dehydration could easily turn into a life-threatening condition. Keep a strict eye on your puppy and be prepared to contact your vet even earlier if he looks lethargic. If he is behaving within normal boundaries, eating normally and wants to play, there should be no reason to worry.

Avoid giving him medicines which are meant for humans at all costs. Many of them have strong side-effects or could even be fatal. If you really want to give your dog something, ask your chemist for a probiotic or electrolytes which are suitable for dogs. Again, do not give him anything which you have bought for your own use.

WORMS

Every dog which is kept properly and is allowed to play and sniff around, who is taken for walks and is allowed to run on fields and grassy patches will get worms sooner or later – that is unavoidable.

With all these activities, your dog will come into contact with the excrement of other dogs and animals. They ingest the worm eggs through the nose or the mouth. Stroking your dog, or allowing him to lick your hand could also pass the eggs onto you and infect you too.

You will not notice that your Newfoundland is suffering from worms until quite late. He will show symptoms of diarrhoea, loss of appetite and itching of the anus. You will probably notice it when your dog "sledges" along the ground, meaning he slides along the ground in the sitting position.

If your dog becomes infested by worms, you will need to make a worm cure immediately. This is a chemical treatment that you can only get from your vet as it is only available on prescription. The amount of repetitions you need to give depends on the compound, the severity of the infestation and the weight of your dog. For this reason, you should follow exactly the directions of your vet.

Today's worm cures are luckily a lot less strenuous than they were a few years ago. Most dogs are almost free of recognisable side-effects. However, your dog will certainly suffer from some changes to his bowel flora through the strong medicine.

Unfortunately, there is no prophylaxis or vaccine against worm infestation at present. This means that a dog can have another bout of worms as soon as 24 hours after finishing the worm treatment.

For this reason, many vets suggest using de-worming treatments regularly – every three to four months – so that the parasites have no chance of survival, even if there are no apparent symptoms.

However, this recommendation is not without its critics as the pharmaceutical companies have not yet carried out any long-term studies about the regular use of their treatments. It is not yet clear how the continual use of their compounds will affect your dog.

If you want to avoid giving your dog worm tablets his whole life, but at the same time be sure that he has not become affected, there is one other effective alternative: A faeces analysis.

For this you should collect stool samples on three consecutive days. A single sample would probably not be enough as you cannot see the worm eggs in every stool. Send the samples to a veterinary medicine laboratory or to your vet and have them analysed for parasites. If the results are positive there is no alternative but to administer another dose of the cure. If the results are negative, you can rest assured and if you wish you can repeat the analysis every three to four months.

This involves a significant amount of effort on the part of the dog owner, but the method is much less strenuous for your dog. An analysis costs between 15 and 30 Euros and has the advantage that your dog does not need to undergo unnecessary medical treatment.

Decide for yourself which method you prefer. You can either treat your dog when he tests positive for the infestation or you give him regular prophylactic treatments, or as a third alternative you can have his stools regularly examined for parasites.

POISONOUS SUBSTANCES AND OTHER PROBLEMATIC THINGS

Did you know that there are many foodstuffs which we humans can eat without problems but which are dangerous, if not fatal for your Newfoundland?

You should never feed your dog any of the following foodstuffs, as they could be life-threatening for him:

- **Avocado**: Dogs could choke if they swallow the stone. There are heated discussions about the effects of the fruit, although there is no scientific proof of the exact dangers.
- **Onions**: The sulphur contained in onions can destroy the red corpuscles in your dog's blood, so never give him your food leftovers. It does not matter if they are raw, cooked or dried.
- **Chocolate & Cocoa**: Cocoa (including chocolate) contains theobromine, which is poisonous for dogs. The darker the chocolate, the greater the proportion of cocoa and therefore the more poisonous the chocolate becomes.

- **Stone fruit**: There is also danger here regarding the stone in the fruit which can cause choking. Most stones are also sharp-edged and can cause injury to the oesophagus, stomach and intestinal mucosa. In some cases, it may even cause intestinal blockage. If your dog bites into the stone, it can release the hydrogen cyanide contained within it, which is also fatal for humans.

- **Grapes and Raisins**: Grapes and raisins contain oxalic acid which can lead to a fatal kidney failure.

- **Raw pork**: The Aujeszky's Disease virus, which can be found in raw pork, is incurable for dogs and is always fatal.

- **Alcohol**: Self-evidently, alcohol can lead to your dog suffering from liver and kidney failure.

- **Caffeine**: Caffeine contains Methyl-xanthines which can be fatal to the nervous system of your dog. Coffee and tea are therefore taboo.

The following foodstuffs are not usually fatal but are poisonous for your four-legged friend and could lead to serious problems:

- **Bacon**: Particularly fatty foods, such as bacon or poultry skin cause metabolic disorders which can cause problems with the kidneys or pancreas.
- **Poultry bones**: Dogs should never be given poultry bones, no matter whether cooked or raw. The thin bones split quickly and can get stuck in their throats.
- **Raw beans**: The toxin Phasin inhibits protein synthesis and can cause the red corpuscles to stick together. If you are going to feed your dog beans, ensure that you cook them first.
- **Raw solanaceous plants**: Raw potatoes, tomatoes and aubergines should never be given to your dog. They can cause diarrhoea, vomiting and brain disorders. The most dangerous part of the plant is the skin. However, these vegetables are no longer a problem once they are cooked.

- **Milk**: As many dogs are have a lactose intolerance, you should not give them any milk which contains lactose.
- **Salt**: Giving salt to your dog can cause them to develop kidney problems.

This was a summary of the main and most dangerous substances for your dog. If you notice that your Newfoundland is not able to cope with other foods, you should stop feeding it to him.

CANCERS

Current studies show that one in every four dogs suffers from a tumour at some time in his life. Every second dog over 10 years of age dies of cancer. This makes cancer undisputedly the most common cause of death in dogs.

It is not exactly clear what causes this, whether it be the consequences of living with humans, increased life expectancy, over-breeding or simply the improved and more intensive veterinary medicine available. What we do know is that some breeds suffer more often with cancer than others. Experts call this a genetic predisposition. Luckily, your Newfoundland is not one of these breeds but also here, cancers are not improbable.

Happily, there are also many therapies which can significantly extend the life expectancy of such dogs. Tumours can be surgically removed and their growth can be inhibited by radiation or chemo therapies. Radio and immune therapies are also among today's remedies which may enable an increase in the life expectancy of your Newfoundland or even cure him.

Dog owners should always weigh the benefits of increasing the length of their dog's life against the quality of his life. Extending his life through surgery or medicines, even if the quality of his life is badly impaired, may help the owner but does not always help his pet. Even if it is difficult, an owner has to be able to make the right choice for his animal.

The best care is better than any therapy, but there are varying opinions about what that should look like. Vets have not been able to establish a link between castration and a reduction in cancer. Castrated animals become just as ill as their "intact" cousins. The only link that vets have been able to establish is that older dogs are more prone to cancer than young ones.

Correct nutrition has also been linked to cancer care. However, this has not been scientifically proven. For this reason, I cannot offer you any recommendations on the best care for your dog in this respect.

That said, I can give you a few tips as to how you can recognise a cancer early. Early detection is very important as tumours spread quickly in dogs and therefore every minute counts in improving the chances of curing him.

Below you will find the most common signs that your Newfoundland could have a tumour:

- **Lumps on or under the skin:** When stroking your dog, be aware of any hardening, lumps or bumps on or under the skin of your Newfoundland. These can be found anywhere on the body.

- **Loss of appetite and unusual loss of weight:** Loss of appetite does not necessarily mean that there is a tumour. However, if it continues over a period of time, you need to have your dog examined. If your dog suddenly loses weight without changing his eating habits, there is definitely a reason to become concerned, as a malignant tumour would change the metabolism of your Newfoundland.

- **Frequent diarrhoea, blood in the vomit or blood in the diarrhoea:** If you see any of these symptoms you should contact your vet. The same applies if your Newfoundland has trouble urinating or defecating.

- **Lethargy or noticeable loss of stamina:** Many owners believe that these symptoms are part of growing old. This is also true, but if the symptoms come suddenly and strongly, you should take notice.
- **Changes in behaviour:** If your Newfoundland suddenly becomes withdrawn or is suddenly particularly clingy, this can also be a symptom.

All these symptoms could be, but are not necessarily, hints that your Newfoundland has cancer. It would not do any harm to have them checked anyway by your vet. Do not panic as these symptoms can also apply to much less serious disorders.

FEVER

The borderline to a fever is not as exact as with us humans. A healthy Newfoundland can have an optimum temperature of between 37.5°C and 39°C.

I would suggest taking your dog's temperature several times while he is healthy, so that you can tell if he is becoming sick. Make sure that he is lying quietly as stress or physical exertion can raise the temperature for a short time.

We speak generally of a "light fever" if the temperature is between 39°C and 40°C, but here there is no need to worry. As I mentioned previously, this could be due to stress or physical exertion.

If his temperature rises above 40°C, you can usually feel the heat coming off your dog. He could start to show outward signs of becoming unwell, such as loss of appetite or general lethargy.

You should contact your vet if his temperature exceeds 41°C. It could be dangerous for your Newfoundland to have a fever for too long.

If his temperature exceeds 42°C this could be very dangerous as the body's own proteins start to clump together – a process which cannot be reversed. At the latest, you should now be contacting your vet or even a pet clinic.

Having a fever does not have to be a bad thing. It is the way that your body destroys pathogens. In addition, it shows that your dog's immune system is working. Fever reduction medicines should not be used unless the fever becomes very high or remains for a long time. Again, never use medicines which are meant for humans, they can be fatal for animals.

How do you measure the temperature on your dog?

The simplest way is with a normal thermometer. I bought one especially for my dogs so that we humans do not have to use the same one. I use a disposable cover to reduce the amount of cleaning necessary afterwards. The best kind of thermometer to buy is one with a flexible tip, they are more comfortable for your dog and at the same you can reduce the danger of injury.

Dampen the thermometer slightly before use and ensure that it is not too cold. Hold your dog's tail firmly and lift it slightly, so that you have more control and safety. Insert the thermometer and wait for the signal before you remove it and check the temperature.

It is best to practise this procedure from puppy age onwards and praise him for standing still. Follow the procedures which you use for other health screening examinations.

If you do not have a thermometer handy, you can recognise a fever by observing the following symptoms:

- Your dog is panting a lot, even though it is not hot.
- The insides of your dog's ears feel warmer than usual, even hot.
- You notice that your dog is drinking much more than usual even though it is not very hot, or he stops drinking altogether.
- When stroking him, he feels warmer than usual, particularly around the nose.
- Your dog generally looks exhausted without having had much physical exertion.

If you see any of the above symptoms, you can assume that your Newfoundland has a fever. Watch him carefully. If you have the feeling that it is getting worse or that it remains for too long a time, you should contact your vet.

VACCINATIONS

The subject of vaccinations is as much of a subject of intense discussion and disagreement as it is with humans. However, in contrast to humans, there is no general compulsory vaccination programme, so it is up to each owner to decide whether to have his dog vaccinated or not.

Of course, every owner wants the best for his dog, but there is a great divide in opinions as to how this can be achieved. A vaccination, depending on the active ingredient, can have a good to very good protection against bacteria as well as viral diseases. However, they do not only protect them from catching them but can also even help to eradicate or at least to repress them. If a pathogen cannot find a host over an extended period of time, the population of this pathogen reduces.

For example, in Germany rabies has been eradicated since 2008. That means that you do not have to have your Newfoundland vaccinated against rabies. However, if you want to travel out of the country with him, you may find it necessary for him to be vaccinated. It is important that you can provide a valid rabies vaccination certificate if your Newfoundland has bitten another animal or even a human. If not, you may find that he has to be euthanised.

The Standing Committee of Veterinary Medicine's Immunisation Committee (known in Germany as the StIKoVet) regularly issues recommendations regarding vaccinations in two forms: Core and non-core vaccinations. Core vaccinations are (according to the StIKoVet) essential vaccinations which are important because a disease has become prevalent for which there are few or no treatments.

Core vaccinations include:

- Rabies
- Distemper
- Infectious Canine Hepatitis
- Parvoviruses
- Leptospirosis

The following vaccinations are less essential and are considered to be non-core:

- Parainfluenza (kennel cough)
- Lyme Borreliosis
- Babesiosis
- Leishmaniasis

- Bordetella bronchiseptica

The non-core vaccinations are also normally only for serious pathogens. However, these disorders often occur regionally and the vaccinations are often not effective for long.

If you decide to have your dog vaccinated, it is important that he gets the primary as well as the subsequent booster injections. The primary vaccination will build up immunity to particular pathogens in your dog's body. The booster injections will ensure continuing protection.

Only healthy dogs should be immunised. Dogs which are sick should not be immunised due to their weakened immune systems. It is also necessary for your dog always to have a thorough examination and a blood test before immunisation.

You should ensure that your puppy receives his primary vaccinations at between 8 and 15 months. The procedure and costs can be determined in consultation with your vet. You should also discuss the appointments for his booster injections early and perhaps arrange for your vet to send you a reminder.

CASTRATION

Many owners expect castration to be a panacea against all kinds of behavioural difficulties, particularly with male dogs. With female dogs, castration is considered more for hygiene reasons, mainly to avoid the inconvenience of her being on heat. In reality, there is a boom in castrations in Germany at the present time and many vets consider it to be a routine intervention, which can be advantageous for many reasons. They give the impression that you are doing a "good thing" for your dog by allowing a castration.

Of course, it is up to you whether you want your dog to be castrated. However, it is important that you think carefully about the subject, considering the pros and cons and what actually happens during castration. You need to have all the information before you can make a decision in the best interests of your dog.

When we speak of castration, we are talking about a veterinary intervention which removes the gonads of your dog. In male dogs it is their testicles and by females the ovaries, fallopian tube, the womb and the cervix are all removed. Castration is a permanent intervention which cannot be reversed. It is carried out under full anaesthetic, which can always carry some risk and there could also be some side effects.

Both the ovaries and testicles produce hormones which are absolutely necessary for the physical and psychological development of your dog, so should never be carried out before puberty. In addition, sexual hormones have a significant influence on the bone structure so castrating an animal too early often leads to joint problems and hip displacement.

The puberty of a Newfoundland usually begins at 7 months (often earlier with female dogs) and can last up to the end of the second or even third year. Contrary to common belief, it does not end when a dog is fully grown. It lasts much longer than that. How long depends not only on the breed but also from environmental factors and it is difficult to generalise. Large dogs, to which the Newfoundland belongs, usually need more time than smaller breeds. Female dogs should never be castrated before they have had their first heat, otherwise they tend to show immature behaviour all their lives.

Many owners believe falsely that they can resolve behavioural problems or prevent cancers with a castration. I can assure you that castration does not resolve behavioural issues. Neither does it help reduce behavioural difficulties on the lead. Nor does it reduce dominance or aggressiveness issues (unless both are due solely to the dog's sex drive). A castration also has no influence at all on territorial protective behaviour.

What many owners do not know is that the sexual behaviour of your dog is already anchored in his brain and cannot be rectified by a castration. A dog which often rubs himself on cushions or on other dogs would continue to do so after a castration. In this case, as with other problematic behaviour, only intensive behavioural training can help.

Many owners also do not know that there are also many unwanted side effects which a castration can cause

- **Obesity**: About 50% of all castrated dogs are obese, which can cause problems such as joint or heart disorders.
- **Personality Change**: The missing hormones can significantly change the personality of your dog, for example he may become lethargic or show general disinterest.

- **Increased ferocity**: Female dogs in particular tend to show increased aggressiveness towards each other.
- **Immature behaviour**: When a dog has been castrated too early, he may never grow up properly and shows immature behaviour all his life.
- **Fur changes:** Almost 30% of female dogs show a dullness in their fur.
- **Incontinence:** About 50% of all female dogs suffer from incontinence when they have been castrated.
- **Ear Infections:** About 30% of all castrated dogs show an increase in ear infections compared to their non-castrated fellows.
- **Bullying**: Other dogs which have not been castrated, and in particular males, will bully a castrated dog.

However, there are also positive effects which can be achieved through a castration. There is, for example, a reliable protection against pregnancies and reproduction generally. Female dogs no longer have their heat which is popular with many owners for hygiene reasons and there will also be no more phantom pregnancies with all their related issues. Male dogs which are castrated no longer have to deal with hormone-induced stress.

There is no scientific proof that the risk of cancers is reduced through castration. Even the feared mammary cancers in female dogs can only be reduced if a dog is castrated before its first heat. Even then, the risk of an uncastrated dog contracting mammary cancer is only 2%.

If you do decide on a castration, I recommend that you shop around as the prices at various vets can vary greatly. For males, the costs can vary between 150 and 250 euros. As the intervention is more extensive, the costs are higher for females and you can pay as much as 450 euros.

More importantly, you should ensure that your dog is thoroughly examined before the castration, because only healthy animals should undergo such an operation. This includes an examination for parasites.

Shortly before the operation you must ensure that your dog does not eat anything for at least 12 hours.

You should not feed your dog even on the evening before the procedure (if it is more than 12 hours before the operation). On the day of the operation, he should not drink anything either.

I have described two methods of castration below, so that you have an idea what happens during the procedure:

- For a male dog, the pubic area is shaved, disinfected and sterilised, ready for castration. The vet pulls the testicles for-wards and opens them with a scalpel. He pulls out the testicles together with the spermatic cord and ties them up. Now he separates the testicles from the spermatic cord and removes them. Lastly, he unbinds the spermatic cord and sews up the wound.
- With a female dog the belly is shaved, disinfected and sterilised. The scalpel cut starts just under the belly button and along the lower abdomen. In most cases, the vet removes the ovaries, fallopian tubes, the womb and the cervix. The inner wound is

sewn up using absorbable sutures and the outer wound is closed with non-absorbable sutures.

After about 10 days, you will have to return to the vet to have the outer sutures removed. The inner sutures will dissolve by themselves.

Directly after the operation, your dog will sleep for another hour or two. When he wakes up, he will be very groggy and will be in a lot of pain. Therefore, it is important that you give him all the painkillers which your vet has prescribed. Dogs are unable to tell us when they are in pain. They are quiet and do not move much; very few of them whine or squeak.

It is up to you whether you want your dog to go through this. I hope to have given you some information in this chapter which can help you with your decision.

DISEASES TYPICAL FOR YOUR BREED

Unfortunately, due to their intensive breeding, Newfoundland dogs suffer from certain conditions specific to their breed. It is advisable that you speak about those concerns with the breeder and find out how previous litters have been affected with them.

The most common of those conditions are as follows:

- **Hip Displacement**: Unfortunately, deformities of the hip have been all too prominent in the German Shepherd and is also now being diagnosed more often with the Newfoundland. The propensity to suffer from hip displacement is mostly genetic, but can also be made worse through false feeding. Young dogs should not start too early with climbing stairs, walking on slippery floors or being
- **Ear Infections:** Dogs with hairy, lop ears, like your Newfoundland, often have insufficient ventilation in them, which can lead to the development of ear infections. For this reason, regular ear care, as

mentioned in the previous chapter, is essential.

- **Gastric Torsion:** Unfortunately, The Newfoundland belongs to the breeds which often suffer from gastric torsion more than others. You will need to watch out for the symptoms mentioned previously and take the necessary precautions. Whether treatment is appropriate or successful depends on how quickly you react.

CHECKLIST: FOR A HEALTHY DOG LIFE

- ☐ Am I feeding my Newfoundland appropriately?
- ☐ Is his weight normal?
- ☐ Does my dog always have access to fresh and clean water?
- ☐ Is my Newfoundland living in a clean environment? (bowls, sleeping place, toys etc.)
- ☐ Is he getting his regular examinations and do I know his normal temperature? Do I attend his appointments conscientiously? (e.g. vaccinations)
- ☐ Am I taking care of my Newfoundland's fur regularly and checking him for ticks?
- ☐ Is my Newfoundland getting enough exercise? Is he being physically challenged? Is he able to frolic, run and play? Am I offering him enough variety on his walks?

- ☐ Am I challenging this clever animal enough intellectually? Does he enjoy working and want more?
- ☐ Can I, in all honesty, say that my Newfoundland is happy with me or would he be better off somewhere else?

CHECKLIST: DOG FIRST AID KIT

- ☐ Medium to combat/heal wound infection (I recommend iodine ointment or Bepanthen – call the vet if in doubt)
- ☐ Dressing material suitable for dogs
- ☐ Paw shoes
- ☐ Waterproof plaster
- ☐ Compresses and bandages
- ☐ Thermometer (with disposable covers)
- ☐ Tick tweezers (or similar tool for removing ticks)
- ☐ Torch
- ☐ Optional blood clotting pen
- ☐ Soft muzzle
- ☐ Disposable gloves
- ☐ Tweezers

- Chapter 5 -

SPECIAL CHAPTER: MAKING YOUR OWN DOG FOOD

I personally take great pleasure in treating my dogs to a homemade snack or meal.

On the following pages I will introduce you to my 10 most favourite recipes so that you can really spoil your four-legged friend, knowing that he is going to enjoy them. In addition to being tasty, they include everything your Newfoundland needs to maintain his health.

Have fun following the recipes!

RECIPE 1: APPLE AND CARROT CRACKERS

Ingredients:

- 1 jar of baby carrot puree (approx. 125g)
- 2 jars of baby apple puree (approx. 125g)
- 200g wholemeal fruit muesli (without sugar, raisins or currents)
- 75g wholemeal flour
- 25g wheat bran
- 50g linseed whole grain
- 2 tbsp. brewer's yeast
- 2 tbsp. organic honey

Preparation:

1. Boil the linseed briefly in a little water until it makes a sticky mass.

2. Mix all the ingredients into the mass, one by one. It may be simpler to blend the muesli into the puree before adding to the linseed mass.

3. Put the mixture into baking moulds. I like to put mine into dog bone-shaped moulds. As an alternative, you could make small balls and lay them onto the baking paper.

4. Bake the crackers at 120°C for about 35-45 minutes.
5. Allow them to cool before you give them to your dog.

With this recipe you are giving your Newfoundland a real vitamin boost. It is also a reasonable snack at only 300 kcal per 100g.

RECIPE 2: WILD POTATO COOKIES

Ingredients:

- 200g potato flour
- 100g minced game (as an alternative you can use beef or chicken hearts)
- 2 eggs
- 2 tbsp rapeseed oil
- Approx. 50ml water

Preparation:

1. Mix all ingredients together.
2. Roll the mixture to about a finger-width in height and cut out the cookies in any shape you wish.
3. Lay the cookies onto baking paper on a baking tray.
4. Bake at 160°C for approx. 25 minutes.
5. Allow to cool after baking, then they are ready to serve.

RECIPE 3: LUNG WITH RICE

Ingredients:

- 250g beef lung (preferably fresh from the butcher)
- 125g round grain rice
- 1 carrot
- 1 banana
- 1 cored apple
- 1 tbsp olive oil

Preparation:

1. Cut the beef lung into small pieces and boil it together with the rice for about 20 minutes in 250ml water.
2. Cut the carrot, banana and apple into small pieces and place in a mixer. Mix together with the olive oil.
3. Add to the rice and lung.
4. Serve when cool.

RECIPE 4: CHICKEN WITH MILLET AND EGG

Ingredients:

- 200g chicken or turkey breast
- 1 boiled egg
- 150g millet
- 1-5 lettuce leaves
- A little olive oil
- 1 tsp fresh parsley

Preparation:

1. Cook the chicken breast thoroughly in a saucepan of water.
2. In the meantime, brown the millet in a pan with the olive oil. Then add a little water and boil it up.
3. Turn the heat onto the lowest setting and allow the millet to simmer for about 12 minutes. Remove and drain.
4. Chop the egg, parsley and lettuce leaves into a bowl and add them to the drained millet.
5. Cut the cooked and cooled meat into bite-sized pieces and mix together with the millet and other ingredients.
6. Allow to cool before serving.

RECIPE 5: RICE MEATBALLS

Ingredients:

- 150g minced beef
- 1 egg
- 40g carrot
- 40g courgette
- 50g rice
- 1 slice wholemeal bread
- 1 slice toast bread

Preparation:

1. Soak the toast bread in water
2. Shred the carrot and courgette
3. Cut the wholemeal bread into small squares
4. Press the surplus water out of the soaked toast bread
5. Mix all ingredients together into a homo-genous mass.
6. Place the mass into a cake tin.
7. Bake at 200°C for 30 minutes.
8. Allow the cake to cook before serving.

RECIPE 6: BEEF MIX

Ingredients:

- 100g beef gullet
- 40g beef spleen
- 40g green beef rumen
- 60g buckwheat
- 1 carrot
- 1/2 cored apple
- 1 tbsp rapeseed oil

Preparation:

1. Cut the gullet into bite-sized pieces and steam at a low temperature.
2. Cut the spleen and rumen into bite-sized pieces but do not steam them.
3. Boil the buckwheat according to the instructions on the packet.
4. Steam the carrot in a bath of water and then puree it.
5. Grate the apple.
6. Mix all the ingredients together with the oil and the healthy beef mix is ready to serve.

RECIPE 7: WILD TURKEY (BARF)

Ingredients:

- 2 turkey necks (preferably fresh from the butcher)
- 40g turkey liver
- 100g turkey goulash
- 40g broccoli
- 1 carrot
- 1 tbsp dried sage
- 1 tbsp rapeseed oil

Preparation:

1. Cut the meat into portions and mix together.
2. Steam the broccoli lightly (raw broccoli can cause flatulence) and cut into small pieces.
3. Grate the carrot
4. Mix the carrot and broccoli and puree them.
5. Fold the sage and oil into the mass.
6. Mix everything together with the meat.

RECIPE 8: ITALIAN TURKEY

Ingredients:

- 300g turkey
- 60g buckwheat noodles
- 1 carrot
- 1 jar of grated beetroot
- 1 tbsp linseed meal
- 1 tbsp rapeseed oil

Preparation:

1. Chop the turkey into rough pieces and steam it gently until cooked.
2. Boil the noodles until soft.
3. Shred the carrot.
4. Mix all ingredients together and allow to cool before serving.

RECIPE 9: DOG ICE-CREAM WITH BANANA AND APPLE

Ingredients:

- 1 banana
- 1 apple
- 1 pack of cottage cheese
- 1 tbsp lactose-free yoghurt

Preparation:

1. Puree the banana and apple (after coring it – you do not need to peel it).
2. Mix the puree with the cottage cheese and yoghurt.
3. Fill small containers with the mass and put them in the freezer.

You can give your dog a real treat in warm weather with this recipe. I chose these two fruits because my dogs love them the most but you can choose any fruits you wish. The ice-cream is meant only to be a treat and should not replace a meal. I always give this to my dogs outside to avoid the mess.

RECIPE 10: DOG ICE-CREAM WITH LIVER SAUSAGE AND OAT FLAKES

Ingredients:

- 1 piece of liver sausage
- 20g oat flakes
- 1 pack cottage cheese
- 1 tbsp lactose-free yoghurt

Preparation:

1. Mix all the ingredients together.
2. Fill small containers with the mass and put them in the freezer.

- Chapter 6 -

CONCLUSION

You've done it! By reading the previous chapters, you have learned a lot about the nutrition and care of your Newfoundland.

This knowledge should not only help you to give your Newfoundland the correct nutrition but will ensure that you keep a cool head should your dog get sick. In addition, you have learned how to take care of your Newfoundland and know that occasional fur brushing is not enough. You know how to examine your dog's eyes and ears, his mouth and paws, his fur and his skin.

You know what you need to watch out for in order to recognise a parasite infestation in good time. In addition, you have learned to understand what is normal for your dog and what you need to have checked by the vet. You have obtained a well-stocked range of care products and a first-aid kit which is suitable for your dog.

You have learned a lot about his nutrition and know what to watch out for when buying pre-prepared foods. You know the advantages and disadvantages of alternative feeding, such as home-cooked foods as well as BARF, vegetarian or vegan foods. You know how much water your dog needs and have learned some simple tricks to motivate him to drink. The recipes you have learned will allow you to treat your dog and make him very happy. My best tip is to give him the ice-cream on very hot days – your Newfoundland will be unbelievably thankful to you!

You both have my sincerest good wishes and I hope that my tips about sicknesses never have to be used! But if so, I am sure that you will now recognise them early enough.

All the best,

Claudia

BOOK RECOMMENDATION FOR YOU

Get the first volume now and find out how to train your Newfoundland puppy.

Newfoundland Dog Training – Dog Training for your Newfoundland puppy

The training of dogs is often...

»... confused with classical dog training drills.

»... only considered necessary for demanding dogs.

»... mocked by other dog owners.

»... replaced by anti-authoritarian methods.

»... considered too difficult to achieve without experience.

What constitutes dog training and what is it good for? And how can you and your Newfoundland profit from it without having any experience?

The most important thing is to understand how a dog sees his world, what is "normal" for him and how you can use this to your advantage. In addition, the characteristics of each breed are significant when you get beyond the basic training phase. Your Newfoundland will show character-ristics which are different to those of a Pug, for example, and this is predominantly what you need to consider during training.

Read about background information, read experience reports and obtain step-by-step instructions and secret tips which are tailor-made for your Newfoundland

Get the second volume now and find out how to train your grown-up Newfoundland!

Newfoundland Training Vol 2 – Dog Training for your grown-up Newfoundland

Dog training is often ...

»... confused with classic basic training of puppies

»... considered only suitable for particularly gifted dogs

»... considered too difficult to achieve without experience

»... replaced by anti-authoritarian methods.

»... considered too difficult to achieve without experience.

What constitutes dog training and what is it good for? And how can you and your Newfoundland profit from it without having any experience?

Do you sometimes have the feeling that your dog has too much energy and does not feel fully stimulated, no matter how often you walk with him? Then dog training is the right thing for you. The simple but very effective methods of physical and mental training that you will read about in this guide will help you to stimulate your Newfoundland, in an appropriate way for his species, while at the same time having fun.

Read about background information, read experience reports and obtain step-by-step instructions and secret tips which are tailor-made for your Newfoundland

Get the new mandala coloring book now with 55 wonderful dog motifs!

MANDALA COLORING BOOK DOGS - 55 animal motifs (dog theme) to colour-in for adults and children

Do you love colouring-in and are you very fond of dogs? Perhaps you are feeling very stressed at the moment and need a moment to relax, a time to switch-off and enjoy your own company?

You can do that with this book. Inside, 55 hand-picked motifs of dogs are waiting for you to bring them to life. Every picture is crafted with great care, creating a wonderful combination of animal drawing and mandalas.

While you are colouring-in, you will notice:

- how you can immerse yourself in the fantastic world of mandalas,
- how your body and mind come to rest and
- how you can leave stress behind you, through mindfulness and patience.

Immerse yourself in the world of mandalas and discover the 55 beautiful and individual dog mandalas contained in this colouring book. As if that is not enough, you will also receive additional 8 mandalas from the fantastic world of our colouring books – free!

Stimulate your imagination and enjoy a moment of peace and tranquillity, just for you!

DID YOU ENJOY MY BOOK?

Now you have read my book, you know how to care for your Newfoundland correctly and how to avoid or deal with possible ailments which may affect him. This is why I am asking you now for a small favour. Customer reviews are an important part of every product offered by Amazon. It is the first thing that customers look at and, more often than not, is the main reason whether or not they decide to buy the product. Considering the endless number of products available at Amazon, this factor is becoming increasingly important.

If you liked my book, I would be more than grateful if you could leave your review by Amazon. How do you do that? Just click the "Write a customer review"-button (as shown below), which you find on the Amazon product page of my book or your orders site:

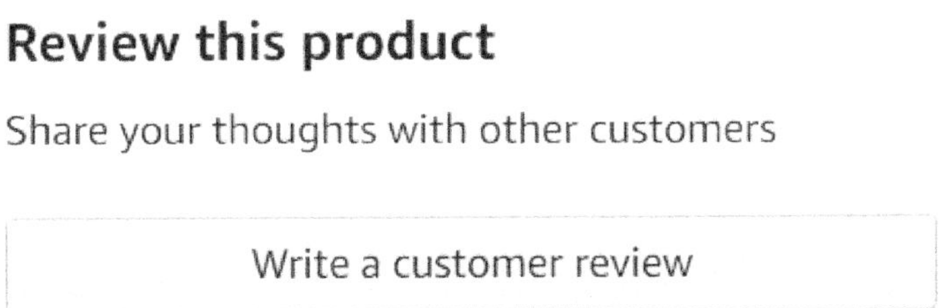

Just write a short review as to whether you particularly liked my book or if there is something I can improve on. It will not take more than 2 minutes, honestly!

Be assured, I will read every review personally. It will help me a lot to improve my books and to tailor them to your wishes.

For this I say to you:

Thank you very much!

Yours
Claudia

SPACE FOR YOUR NOTES

REFERENCES

Winkler, Sabine: So lernt mein Hund: Der Schlüssel für die erfolgreiche Erziehung und Ausbildung. 3rd edition. Stuttgart: Kosmos Verlag

Neufundländer: d. Neufundländer u. Landseer-Neufundländer von Ippen, Heinrich 1985

Newfoundland Puppy Training Book for Newfoundland Puppies 2018 Karen Douglas Kane

Neufundländer und Landseer: Jubiläumsausgabe Taschenbuch 2006 Victor Goerttler

Neufundländer 2001 von Wulf A Gewert, Wolfgang Dettlaff

Neufundländer heute (Das besondere Hundebuch) 1999 von Hedd Richards, Del RichardsRütter, Martin; Buisman, Andrea: Hundetraining mit Martin Rütter. 2. Auflage. Stuttgart: Kosmos Verlag 2014

Rütter, Martin; Buisman, Andrea: Hundetraining mit Martin Rütter. 2nd edition. Stuttgart: Kosmos Verlag 2014

Fichtlmeier, Anton: Suchen und Apportieren: Denksport für Hunde. 1st edition. Stuttgart: Kosmos Verlag 2015

Schlegl-Kofler, Katharina: Apportieren: Das einzigartige Step-by-Step-Programm. 1st edition. München: Gräfe und Unzer Verlag 2018

Rütter, Martin; Buismann, Andrea: Hunde beschäftigen mit Martin Rütter: Spiele für jedes Mensch-Hund-Team. 1st edition. Stuttgart: Kosmos Verlag 2016

Theby, Viviane; Hares, Michaela: Das große Schnüffelbuch: Nasenspiele für Hunde (Das besondere Hundebuch). 2nd edition. Nerdlen/Daun: Kynos Verlag 2011

Schmidt-Röger, Heike: Das grosse Praxishandbuch. 6th edition. München: Gräfe und Unzer Verlag 2013

Laukner, Anna: Hunde pflegen: Einfach – richtig – schön. 1st edition. Stuttgart: Eugen Ulmer Verlag 2009

Kohtz-Walkemeyer, Marianne: BARF für Hunde: Den besten Freund gesund ernähren. 1st edition. München Gräfer und Unzer Verlag 2014

Dr. Hartmann, Michael: Patient Hund: Krankheiten vorbeugen, erkennen, behandeln. 1st edition. Reutlingen: Oertel & Spörer Verlag 2015

Dr. med. vet. Bucksch, Martin: Gesunde Ernährung für Hunde: Fertigfutter oder selbstgemacht – gesundes Futter für jeden Hund. 1st edition. Stuttgart: Kosmos Verlag 2017

Zentek, Jürgen: Hunde richtig füttern. 3rd edition. Stuttgart: Eugen Ulmer Verlag 2012

DISCLAIMER

1st Edition

 Publisher: GbR, Martin Seidel und Corinna Krupp, Bachstraße 37, 53498 Bad Breisig, Germany, email: info@expertengruppeverlag.de, Cover photo: www.depositphotos.com. The information provided within this book is for general information purposes only. It does not represent any recommendation or application of the methods mentioned within. The information in this book does not purport to imply or guarantee its completeness, accuracy, or topicality. This book in no way replaces the competent recommendations of, or care given by, a dog school. The author and publisher do not assume and hereby disclaims any liability for damages or disruption caused by the use of the information given herein.

Printed in Great Britain
by Amazon

25775192R00106